ASIE CENTRALE
CENTRAL ASIA
ZENTRALASIEN

In the same series:

ANATOLIA I (From the origins to the end of the 2nd millennium B.C.)	U. Bahadır Alkım, Professor at the University of Istanbul
ANATOLIA II (1st millennium B.C.)	Henri Metzger, Professor at the University of Lyons
BYZANTIUM	Antoine Bon, Professor at the University of Lyons
CELTS AND GALLO-ROMANS	Jean-Jacques Hatt, Professor at the University of Strasbourg
CENTRAL AMERICA	
CHINA	Madeleine Paul-David, Professor at the Ecole du Louvre, Paris
CRETE	Nicolas Platon, former Superintendent of Antiquities, Crete; Director of the Acropolis Museum, Athens
CYPRUS	Vassos Karageorghis, Director of the Archaeological Museum, Nicosia
EGYPT	Jean Leclant, Professor at the Sorbonne, Paris
THE ETRUSCANS	Raymond Bloch, Professor at the Sorbonne, Paris
GREECE I (Mycenaean and geometric periods)	Nicolas Platon, former Superintendent of Antiquities, Crete; former Director of the Acropolis Museum, Athens
GREECE II (Post-geometric periods)	François Salviat, Professor at the University of Aix-en-Provence
INDIA	Maurizio Taddei, Inspector of Oriental Art and Archaeology, Rome
INDOCHINA	Bernard P. Groslier, Curator of Historical Monuments, Angkor; Director of Archeological Research at the Ecole Française d'Extrême-Orient
INDONESIA	Bernard P. Groslier, Curator of Historical Monuments, Angkor; Director of Archaeological Research at the Ecole Française d'Extrême-Orient
MESOPOTAMIA	Jean-Claude Margueron, Agrégé of the University; Member of the French Institute of Archaeology of Beirut

MEXICO	Jacques Soustelle
PERSIA I (From the origins to the Achaemenids)	Jean-Louis Huot, Agrégé of the University; Member of the French Archaeological School in Jerusalem
PERSIA II (From the Seleucids to the Sassanids)	Vladimir Lukonin, Curator at the Hermitage Museum, Leningrad
PERU	Rafael Larco Hoyle†, Director of the Rafael Larco Herrera Museum, Lima
PREHISTORY	Denise de Sonneville-Bordes, Ph. D.
ROME	Gilbert Picard, Professor at the Sorbonne, Paris
SOUTH CAUCASUS	Boris B. Piotrovsky, Director of the Hermitage Museum, Leningrad
SOUTH SIBERIA	Mikhail Gryaznov, Curator at the Hermitage Museum, Leningrad
SYRIA-PALESTINE I (Ancient Orient)	Jean Perrot, Head of the French Archaeological Mission in Israel
SYRIA-PALESTINE II (Classical Orient)	Michael Avi Yonah, Professor at the University of Jerusalem
THE TEUTONS	R. Hachmann, Professeur at the University of Saarbrücken
URARTU	Boris B. Piotrovsky, Director of the Hermitage Museum, Leningrad

ARCHAEOLOGIA MVNDI

Series prepared under the direction of
Jean Marcadé, Professor of Archaeology
at the University of Bordeaux

ALEKSANDR BELENITSKY

CENTRAL
ASIA

Translated from the Russian by James Hogarth

54 illustrations in colour; 89 illustrations in black and white

THE WORLD PUBLISHING COMPANY CLEVELAND
AND NEW YORK

CONTENTS

		Page
Preface		11
Introduction		15
	The Country and the Archaeological Remains	15
	The First Investigations	16
	Investigations since 1917	18
	Present-day Methods	20
Chapter I	*Prehistoric Central Asia*	23
	The Palaeolithic Period	23
	Teshik-Tash	23
	Aman-Kutan, Karatau, Zaraut-Say	24
	Progress in the Mesolithic Period	25
	The Neolithic and the Bronze Age in Southern Turkmenia	26
	Anau	26
	The Dzhebel Cave	27
	Dzheytun	27
	Namazga-Depe, Geoksyur, Kara-Depe	28
	General	30
	Other Civilisations of the Neolithic and the Bronze Age	45
	The Cultures of Khorezm	45
	The Hissar Culture	46
	The Kayrakkum Culture	47
	The Chust Culture	47

		Page
The Zaman-Baba Culture		48
Conclusions		49
Chapter II	*Central Asia in the Early Historical Periods*	51
	The Achaemenid Period	51
	The Ancient Sources	51
	The Historical Data	53
	The Oxus Treasure	54
	The Archaeology of Urban Sites	54
	Sacian Tombs	56
	The Greek Period	57
	Alexander's Conquest	58
	The Greco-Bactrian Kingdom	59
	Urban Sites in Bactriana	74
	Other Urban Sites	76
Chapter III	*Central Asia in the Kushan Period*	93
	The Historical Framework	93
	Literary and Epigraphical Sources	94
	The Economic and Cultural Context	97
	The Archaeological Evidence	98
	The Ayrtam Frieze	98
	The Ruins of Khalchayan	99
	Toprak-Kala	102

		Page
	Tali-Barzu	103
	The Kurgan Cemeteries	104
	The Tup-Khona Cemetery	105
Chapter IV	*From the Kushans to the Arab Conquest*	109
	The Historical Data	109
	Hephthalites and Turks	110
	Economic, Social and Religious Life	111
	The Arrival of the Arabs	114
	Post-Kushan Archaeology	115
	The Fort of Balalyk-Tepe	116
	The Shrines of Ak-Beshim and Kuva	137
	The Buddhist Monastery of Adzhina-Tepe	139
	The Palace of Varakhsha	142
	Pendzhikent	154
	Architecture	156
	Material Life	159
	Written Records	185
	Art	186
	Subjects and Themes	187
Chapter V	*The Main Problems*	191
	Problems of Acculturation and Socio-economic Problems	191
	Problems of Art History	209

  Page

            Problems in the History of Religion 214

Synoptic Chronological Tables 220

Notes 225

Select Bibliography 227

Map 236

List of Illustrations 239

Index 247

PREFACE

*I*n spite of the remarkable progress it has made, particularly since the last war, the archaeology of Central Asia has not yet received the attention it merits from the general public of western Europe. The most widely available works of reference have little to say about these distant regions with their difficult and outlandish place-names. All the more reason, therefore, for including a volume on this subject in the Archaeologia Mundi series.

Among the varied and constantly changing aspects of contemporary archaeology, the archaeology of Central Asia offers some striking and distinctive features.

The problems in this field are related to the comparative scarcity of written sources and to the fact that for the most part they are of external origin, and thus of a secondary nature, for the periods of ancient history which we are accustomed to refer to as classical. Whereas in the Mediterranean area and the Near East epigraphy and literature provide an immediate and detailed commentary on the archaeological horizons discovered by excavation, in Central Asia local inscriptions are still exceptional and we must usually rely for our documentation on the study of coins. Our knowledge of the various civilisations thus comes mainly from their material remains, not only for periods earlier than the Iron Age but almost until the end of the Hellenistic period; and yet before the Kushan period the territories with which we are concerned had formed part of the Achaemenid empire and later of the empire of Alexander and the Seleucid kingdom, and had seen the establishment of the Greco-Bactrian state.

Since the archaeology of Central Asia is mainly "monumental", its methods have been perfected principally in the exploration of the town sites and the large cemeteries of which so many lie concealed in the soil of this region of tepes and kalas. The layout of the towns, the plan of the citadels, the disposition of the sanctuaries, the architectural techniques, the carved or painted decoration of the buildings—these are our main sources of evidence on the stage of social development reached in the different periods, on their economic level, their cultural evolution, their contacts with neighbouring countries, the influences which they received and passed on to others. In this field Soviet scholars have achieved some spectacular successes—at Afrosiab, Nisa, Khalchayan, Toprak-Kala and Varakhsha. More than a thousand years of history, from the Achaemenid period to the time of the Hephthalites and the Turks, are brought before our eyes in concrete form by the imposing remains discovered by the archaeologists; and sometimes we see a miraculous resurrection of the past on a site abandoned at the time of the Arab invasion and forgotten until its rediscovery in our own day, as at the town of Pendzhikent near Samarkand.

The results obtained in this area are of exceptional importance for the general history of civilisation. As a nodal point on the ancient trade routes—on the farthest confines of the Near Eastern empires but on the "Silk Road" from the Far East, in contact with India from a very early period but with a convenient route to the north by way of the steppes—Central Asia offers particularly favourable opportunities for studying the phenomena of acculturation, contamination and syncretism. As archaeology enlarges our knowledge of the earliest farming communities we are confronted with a whole series of questions—on the origin of social structures, the principles of class differentiation, the initial stimuli towards material progress, the relationships between the nomadic and the settled population, the consequences of the migrations of peoples. The discovery in so many different areas of remains of monumental art makes it necessary to reconsider or elaborate on certain over-simplified theories about the spread of the great classical civilisations and the formation of "hybrid" styles; in particular, there is now no doubt about the great importance of the Kushan period in the development of the various schools of art which flourished in Central Asia. Finally, as evidence accumulates on the peaceful co-existence of several different religions on the town sites of the pre-Islamic period, with the iconographical contaminations and the syncretisms which this entailed, we obtain an interesting insight into the religious toleration of the ancient world.

J.M.

We should like to express our gratitude to Mr Boris B. Piotrovsky, Director of the Hermitage Museum, Leningrad, for his constant readiness to give us advice and assistance.

Our thanks are also due to Mr Boris Marshak, Curator of the Department of Central Asian Archaeology in the Hermitage Museum, for the help he gave us during the taking of photographs for the illustrations.

Finally we are grateful to the Archaeological Institute of the Academy of Science of the U.S.S.R. in Leningrad and to the Institute of History of the Academy of Science of the Tadzhik S.S.R. for so readily making available to us the material we required.

INTRODUCTION

In contemporary Soviet usage the geographical term "Central Asia" has a rather different connotation from the term as it is normally used in western Europe. It includes the territory of the Uzbek, Tadzhik, Turkmenian and Kirghiz Republics and the southern part of the Kazakh Republic, but excludes eastern Turkestan, Mongolia and Tibet, which are covered by the western European term.

Central Asia is a land of sharp geographical contrasts. The greater part of the area is occupied by high mountain systems or great deserts which are unfavourable for human settlement; but many of its river valleys, with their fertile loess soil, have been occupied by settled populations since the remotest times, and the foothills and steppes offer excellent conditions for stock-rearing. Archaeological investigation has established that man appeared in Central Asia as early as the Palaeolithic period and has occupied the area continuously since then.

The Country and the Archaeological Remains

Geographical conditions in Central Asia are similar in many respects to those of the Near Eastern countries, and the cultural development of the two areas also shows many similarities. In particular the lack of timber led to the use of the easily worked local loess for building from the earliest times, and this in turn determined the whole archaeological landscape of the country. When the old settlements were abandoned by their occupants they rapidly reverted to hillocks or mounds of more or less regular outline, barely distinguishable from natural mounds, which merge easily into the landscape. Only in the western parts of Central Asia, in the desert areas, has the archaeological landscape a more distinctive character. In Kharezm (Chorasmia) and southern Turkmenia the picturesque ruins of old city walls with projecting towers and the remains of fortresses and other more modest structures can still be seen standing above the ground.

The local inhabitants call these ruins by the name of *tepe* or *kala*, corresponding to the *tells* of Mesopotamia; and indeed the term "tell" is also occasionally met with in Central Asia. The original names of these settlements are almost invariably forgotten, and the only suggestion of their great antiquity comes from the occurrence in the modern names of such terms as *kafir*, "unbeliever" (in the same sense as *gyaur*, found in English as "giaour") or *mug*, or the names of mythical characters from the epics such as Afrosiab or Key-Kobad-Shakh. As a rule, however, the names of these sites, like most of the local place names, are derived from the external appearance of the mounds and give no indication of their antiquity.

The *tepe* or *kala* is the most characteristic monument of human settlement throughout Central Asia. In the Semirechye (the "Seven Rivers" region to the south of Lake Balkhash) the term *turt-kul* is also frequently met with.

In many parts of Central Asia, particularly in the foothill areas, groups of *kurgans* (small artificial burial mounds or barrows) are of common occurrence, often forming cemeteries of considerable extent. In some of these cemeteries a definite pattern can be detected, the mounds being arranged in rows or groups of varying degrees of regularity.

The First Investigations

The remains of antiquity in Central Asia aroused interest among Russian scholars from an early stage. Even before Samarkand was occupied by Russian forces (1868) the Imperial Archaeological Commission despatched an expedition from St Petersburg under the leadership of the orientalist and numismatist P.I. Lerkh, who carried out excavations in 1867 on the site of the late settlement at Dzhankent in the lower Syr-Darya valley. The first reports on these excavations aroused exaggerated expectations of the wealth of material to be revealed: indeed the well-known critic V.V. Stasov prophesied that the site would be "the Pompeii of Turkestan", although in fact the very commonplace material found there gave no basis for expectations of this kind.

The architectural monuments of Central Asia, particularly those of Samarkand, made a deep impression on the Russian public, largely through the intermediary of the paintings of the artist Vasily Vereshchagin. Interest was also aroused in the extensive ancient site of Afrosiab, near Samarkand, on which the efforts of the archaeologists were now principally concentrated. It is unnecessary to relate the whole history of the archaeological investigation of Afrosiab, but we may refer briefly to some features of the work.

Excavation was begun at Afrosiab in 1875, and it is fair to say that it has continued, with lengthy interruptions, to the present day[1]. At first the work was not in particularly competent hands, being carried out by officers of the Russian forces, but thereafter the excavations were directed by the prominent Russian archaeologist N.I. Veselovsky; and from the beginning of this century until the 1920s systematic excavation was carried out at Afrosiab under the direction of V.L. Vyatkin.

Judged by the standards of present-day archaeology, however, the results produced by the investigation of this very complex site are unsatisfactory. The methods employed, based on the cutting of narrow trenches through the site, gave the excavators no opportunity to gain an understanding of the various building horizons, the succession of levels and their dating — that is, of achieving the most elementary objectives of archaeological investigation. But with all their defects the excavations at Afrosiab were of considerable importance. They yielded a large quantity of material — glass, pottery of all kinds, including the high quality glazed ware which is known as Afrosiab ware, and large numbers of small terracotta pieces belonging to the pre-Moslem period.

An important event of the early 1890s was the investigation of the ruins of the ancient city of Merv. These were the subject of a monograph by V.A. Zhukovsky, "The Ruins of Old Merv", a valuable study which brought together a rich collection of material from the written sources. The archaeological part of the book, however, was confined to a descriptive account of the visible remains.

As the area became better known public interest in its antiquities increased, and the first antiquarian societies or amateur archaeologists' associations began to make their appearance. The first of these, founded at Tashkent in 1894, was a very active body which continued in existence until 1916. During these years twenty volumes of its *Transactions* were published, containing many articles and communications on archaeology. The most interesting of these were concerned with the "ossuaries" which are such a characteristic feature of Central Asian archaeology.

The Archaeological Society of Ashkhabad was less active, producing only two volumes of *Transactions*.

Museums were opened in many towns, and these devoted some attention to archaeological material. The Samarkand Museum, founded in 1896, provided a home for the extensive collection of material from the excavations at Afrosiab[2].

In any account of archaeological work in Central Asia in the period before the 1917 Revolution mention must be made of the excavations of two mounds at Anau, near Ashkhabad, carried out by an American expedition from the University of Philadelphia led by R. Pumpelly (1904) and by W. Schmidt's expedition (1905). On these sites remains dating from the Bronze Age were discovered; but the excavations were no more than an episode in the history of Central Asian archaeology, and for many years were not followed up.

Investigations since 1917

The profound social changes which followed the October Revolution were reflected in the organisation of the archaeological service. Special committees with responsibility for directing archaeological work were established by the new Commissariats of Education, their main concern being the preservation and restoration of the numerous surface remains of the mediaeval period in Central Asia.

The 1920s were not a propitious time for archaeological investigation in the proper sense of the term, i.e., for field excavations. Reference must, however, be made to the work carried out at Termez in 1926-28 by an expedition from the Moscow Scientific Centre led by B.P. Denike, and to the excavation in 1928 of a cemetery in the Semirechye dating from the early centuries of our era (M. V. Voevodsky, M.P. Gryaznov).

A new stage in the archaeological investigation of Central Asia began in the thirties of this century. Two important finds, made quite by chance, heralded further discoveries and gave a powerful stimulus to the development of archaeology. In the spring of 1932 the first documents in the Sogdian language to be found in Central Asia were discovered in the ruins of the ancient fortress of Kala-i-Mug in the Zeravshan mountain range; and in the autumn of the same year a stone slab carved in relief was discovered lying in the bed of the river at the small settlement of Ayrtam on the right bank of the Amu-Darya. It became evident that the soil of Central Asia concealed a great wealth of remains from the remote past, which could be recovered only by planned and systematic archaeological investigation.

These investigations of the 1930s were carried out by expeditions organised by scientific institutions in Moscow, Leningrad and Tashkent. In 1934 there was the Zeravshan Expedition led by Professor A.Y. Yakubovsky; and in 1936 the Termez Expedition, under the leadership of M.E. Masson, began its work.

In 1937, under the direction of S.P. Tolstov, the archaeological investigation of the territory of Khorezm was begun. At the same time (1936-40) a number of expeditions led by A.N. Bernshtam carried out investigations in large areas in the Semirechye and southern Kazakhstan. From the start the results produced by these expeditions were impressive, and some of them were sensational (e.g., the Teshik-Tash cave, Varakhsha, etc.). During the second world war the scale of archaeological work in Central

Asia was, of course, drastically reduced; but mention must be made of the interesting results produced by excavations carried out in 1943-44 on the site of the Farkhad hydro-electric station (near the town of Begovat, on the left bank of the Syr-Darya), and of the excavation of the Shirin-Say cemetery and the settlement of Munchak-Tepe under the direction of V.F. Gaydukevich.

After the end of the war archaeological investigations in Central Asia were resumed on a considerably increased scale. The Khorezm Expedition extended the geographical scope of its work to take in the lower Syr-Darya valley (Kazakhstan). Two large permanent expeditions were re-established — the Tadzhik Expedition (at first known as the Sogdo-Tadzhik Expedition) under the direction of A.Y. Yakubovsky, and the Southern Turkmenian Expedition under the direction of M.E. Masson. In Kirghizia and southern Kazakhstan excavations were carried out by expeditions led by A.N. Bernshtam.

In the 1940s and early 1950s Academies of Science were established in all the Soviet Republics of Central Asia, and attached to these Academies were Historical Institutes with archaeological departments. The function of these departments was to carry out the orderly and systematic investigation of the remains of the past throughout the territory of the various Republics. The selection of sites for study was in practice often determined by extraneous circumstances — for example, by the development of building and civil engineering projects. (Under Soviet law the authorities responsible for any such operations — e.g., the construction of a canal or a hydro-electric scheme — are required to pay for the examination and excavation of any archaeological remains within the construction site).

Present-day Methods

In order to solve the fundamental historical problems with which it is concerned, archaeology has had to develop new methods of investigation.

The conception of archaeology as a quest for beautiful and spectacular objects is a thing of the past. The archaeologists of today are concerned to extract the maximum amount of information from the material they study. The techniques adopted, for example, by de Morgan in his excavations at Susa — where in order to reach the lower pre-Achaemenian levels he was looking for he destroyed all the levels above them — are no longer conceivable. Nor can we now tolerate the methods described by Sir Leonard Woolley at Ur, where, in order to induce his workmen to surrender the gold objects found in the course of excavation, he was obliged to offer them higher prices than the dealers were prepared to pay: in other words, the excavations were carried on without proper supervision by qualified archaeologists. Nowadays excavation is organised on very different principles: in each section of the site the work is under constant observation by an archaeologist or a trained technician. The scale of operations and the labour force employed are determined mainly by the number of qualified staff available to supervise and record the progress of the work. This requirement, of course, inevitably slows up the process of excavation — and, unfortunately, adds to its cost.

The continuance of excavation for a number of years on the same site — particularly on sites with a long history of occupation — is a characteristic feature of contemporary archaeological work. The discovery of works of art such as wall paintings, carved wood ornament and clay sculpture makes it necessary to provide facilities on the spot so that they can be given conservative treatment and prepared for removal to properly equipped restoration workshops. The history of archaeology records all too many cases in which material of this kind perished irretrievably for lack of expert care. A recent example of this is the loss of the wall paintings of Susa; and there have been many similar instances in the past. Excellent results have been achieved by the preservation technique developed at the Hermitage Museum, Leningrad, by the artist-restorer P.I. Kostrov and his colleagues — a method based on the use of a colourless synthetic resin (polybutylme-tacrylate).

The scale on which excavation has been conducted has led to the accumulation of vast quantities of material. In the circumstances of Central Asia this consists mainly of pottery objects and the remains of human and animal bones. Publication of this material in the normal form of a catalogue or inventory does little to advance knowledge, and in practice this great store of material has not in itself proved a productive source of additional information. In recent years, however, some very promising attempts have been made to apply statistical methods to the study of this evidence, and these have produced findings of far-reaching historical significance. The use of computers for this purpose is also projected. In general, the quest for new methods in archaeology has been following the same directions in the Soviet Union as in other countries.

Archaeological work in Central Asia has been greatly facilitated, particularly in areas which are now under desert, by the use of air photography. This is particularly effective, for example, in revealing ancient irrigation systems. And the use of methods of investigation developed by the natural sciences (radiocarbon dating, pollen analysis, etc.) has become normal archaeological practice.

PREHISTORIC CENTRAL ASIA

The Palaeolithic Period

One of the distinctive features of contemporary archaeology is its concern with the origins of human civilisation and the earliest stages of its development. In every continent, in both the Old and the New World, remarkable advances have been made in the study of the Palaeolithic period, and much valuable work has been published in this field.

The archaeology of Central Asia has not been backward in this respect. Active prospecting for remains of the Palaeolithic in Central Asia began in the 1930s, and was not long in producing important results.

Teshik-Tash

One of the most remarkable discoveries was made in 1938 in the Baysun Mountains (south-east of Termez), where the first Palaeolithic (Mousterian) occupation site in Central Asia was discovered in a cave at Teshik-Tash. The discovery was made by local archaeologists, and the site was excavated by A.P. Okladnikov, then at the beginning of his career as a student of the antiquities of Siberia.

In addition to a considerable quantity of stone implements and animal bones the discoveries in the Teshik-Tash cave included the skeleton of a boy of 8 or 9 years of age *(Plate 1)*. He had been buried under the overhang of the cave in a shallow pit covered with the horns of mountain goats. Particular interest attached to the skull of this Neanderthal boy, which was in a fair state of preservation. This was only the second occasion on which, throughout the whole area of the Soviet Union, remains dating from such a remote period (thirty to forty thousand years before our era) had come to light.

This find aroused intense interest in the learned world. In the words of the great American expert A. Hrdlička, the discovery "halves the distance from the western Neanderthalers to Peking Man."[3] Certain other data and observations yielded by the excavations in the Teshik-Tash cave are also of considerable significance: for example, the specially built stone hearth at the entrance to the cave, and the fact that the boy had been deliberately buried, which gave rise to lively discussion among scholars. In the opinion of the best authorities a burial of this kind is evidence that the men of this period had already developed some conception of an after-life.

The discoveries at Teshik-Tash provided a stimulus to further search for remains of the Palaeolithic period. Since then many similar sites have been found in Central Asia, and archaeologists in all the Central Asian Soviet Republics have been continuing with prospecting and research in this field.

Aman-Kutan, Karatau, Zaraut-Say

The Palaeolithic remains which have been discovered include some which are earlier than Teshik-Tash, and some which are later. One or two of the most important of these may be briefly mentioned. Excavations have been in progress for many years, under the direction of D.N. Lev, in a large limestone cave (Middle Palaeolithic) at Aman-Kutan, 28 miles south of Samarkand, near the Takhta-Karacha pass. North of Chimkent, in the Karatau Mountains, occupation sites belonging to the Lower Palaeolithic were discovered by the young Kazakh archaeologist Kh. Alpysbaev.

In addition to these occupation sites some interesting rock paintings dating from the same period have been discovered. Among these are the paintings found at Zaraut-Say in the Baba-Tag Mountains, 60 miles east of Termez. There are more than 200 paintings in red ochre representing animals, the most interesting being a scene showing hunters dressed in skins shooting wild oxen with bows and arrows. To an earlier period belong the paintings in the Shakhty cave in the Pamirs, discovered by V.A. Ranov. These also include a hunting scene in which the hunter is disguised as a bird. An interesting point is that his arrows are shown either on the animal's body or in close proximity to it. Ranov compares these paintings with the well-known drawings of animals on the walls of the Palaeolithic Grotte de Niaux in the Ariège (south-western France). Pictures of this kind are associated with the earliest forms of magic.

Year by year archaeologists are continually finding new Palaeolithic occupation sites, which make it clear that many tens of thousands of years before our era human settlement was extending over Central Asia; and yet, not so long ago, this suggestion was rejected by many scholars.

Progress in the Mesolithic Period

Between the Palaeolithic and the Neolithic archaeologists now recognise an intermediate period, the Mesolithic or Middle Stone Age, which is of great significance in the development of primitive society, particularly in the Near East.

Chronologically this period is of relatively short duration — no more than a few thousand years. Its beginning is put at about the 10th millennium B.C. An important development in the Mesolithic period was the invention of the bow; and the men of this period also learned to make delicately fashioned stone arrowheads. This advanced long-range weapon was destined to have a long and successful career, remaining in use until it was superseded by fire-arms in the late Middle Ages.

In some parts of the Near East during the early stages of the Neolithic period man was no longer content with the supplies of food which nature provided — the wild animals he hunted and the wild plants he harvested — and began to grow useful crops for himself and to domesticate certain animals. This process — the beginnings of agriculture and stock-rearing — led to profound changes in the whole structure and way of life of human society. Archaeologists concerned with Central Asia devote much attention to the study of a period which is regarded as transitional between a food-gathering and a food-producing form of economy.

The Neolithic and the Bronze Age in Southern Turkmenia

Within the territory of Central Asia the most favourable natural conditions for a transition of this kind were to be found in southern Turkmenistan. The discoveries in this area belonging to the transitional period, and to an even greater extent those belonging to the following period when a civilisation based on agriculture and already showing Bronze Age characteristics reached a high level of achievement, have rightly taken a prominent place in the archaeology not only of Central Asia but of the Near East as a whole.

Anau

The study of these cultures began as early as 1904-5 with the excavation of two mounds near the *aul* (village) of Anau, 7 miles south-east of Ashkhabad. The excavations, carried out by an American expedition headed by R. Pumpelly, gave rise at the time to some rather exaggerated claims. For a time the Anau culture was regarded as perhaps the oldest farming culture in the world, while southern Turkmenia was pronounced to be the oldest centre of development of cultivated varieties of wheat.

This over-estimate of the significance of Anau was due to an incorrect and unduly early dating of the site (9th millennium B.C.), which in turn resulted from unsatisfactory excavation techniques. The narrow trenches which were cut through the mounds did not allow the excavators to identify the levels with sufficient accuracy — quite apart from the fact that they overlooked many important details. In fact from the point of view of Central Asian archaeology the Anau excavations were of merely episodic significance, and after the American expedition had completed their investigations the work was not resumed.

The systematic study of the cultures of the Mesolithic, Neolithic and Bronze Age, indeed, did not begin until the 1930s, and was intensively pursued after the second world war. We may briefly review the most important discoveries in this field.

The Dzhebel Cave

In 1938 a cave was excavated in the Dzhebel Hills near Krasnovodsk, at the western extremity of Turkmenia, showing in its successive levels a gradual transition from the Mesolithic to the early stages of the Neolithic. With the help of radiocarbon dating the age of the latest phase was fixed within the 5th and 6th millennia B.C., and accordingly the Mesolithic occupation, which lay below this, was dated somewhat earlier. As a result the material found at Dzhebel has provided a chronological standard for the dating of other sites belonging to the same periods, a large number of which have been discovered in southern Turkmenia in recent years. The excavations at the Dzhebel Cave have also made it possible to establish the relationships between the Mesolithic and Early Neolithic cultures of Turkmenia and similar remains in the Caspian area of Iran and as far afield as Palestine.

Dzheytun

The name of this site is now associated with the culture of the earliest farmers in Central Asia, following the discovery of a sizeable farming settlement here. The credit for its discovery is due to A.A. Marushchenko, an archaeologist who has been responsible for finding many ancient sites in southern Turkmenistan. Dzheytun lies on a low hill 20 miles north-west of Ashkhabad, and is now surrounded by the sand-hills of the

Kyzyl-Kum Desert. The excavation of the site, which occupies an area of roughly an acre, was begun by B.A. Kuftin and completed by V.M. Masson, now one of the most active practitioners of Central Asian archaeology. Here the remains of 35 separate dwelling houses were excavated, built of round blocks of sun-dried clay—the forerunners of the adobe bricks which were to be the principal building material of Central Asia throughout many succeeding centuries. The houses were small in size, each consisting of a single room with an area of up to 215 square feet.

At Dzheytun a Neolithic flint industry still prevails. Among the most interesting of the many flint instruments discovered on the site are the blades, consisting of flakes sharpened on one side, which were inserted into bone sickles. The function of these implements was revealed by the discovery of the sickles themselves and of many impressions left by wheat and barley grains in the clay from which the pottery was moulded. The excavators also found stone querns used for grinding corn into meal or flour. The pottery was made by hand without the use of a wheel, but already showed a primitive form of decoration in the shape of parallel lines painted in ochre.

The animal bones found in the excavations were of great interest, showing that the process of domesticating certain animals such as the sheep had already begun. Hunting, however, was still an important element in the way of life practised here.

Dzheytun is now recognised as the oldest evidence of an agricultural civilisation in Central Asia, comparable in its cultural level with such well-known sites as Jarmo in north-western Iran and Al Ubaid in southern Mesopotamia.

Namazga-Depe, Geoksyur, Kara-Depe

These sites are characteristic of the later stages of development of the farming cultures, and already belong to the Chalcolithic (Eneolithic) period and the

Bronze Age. They are by no means the only sites known, but they are the sites which have been most thoroughly investigated. Their discovery and excavation has been the work of a large number of archaeologists of both the older and the younger generations.

Namazga-Depe is a large hill, covering an area of over 170 acres, near the railway station of Kaakhka, south-east of Ashkhabad. It was investigated in the 1920s by an irrigation engineer, D.D. Bukinich, who was able to establish its outstanding importance. Bukinich paid particular attention to the methods of irrigation used by the early agriculturists of southern Turkmenistan, and was even able to trace the pattern of successive improvements in technique. Thus the earliest type of irrigation farming was the method known as estuary or *liman* irrigation, in which crops were sown at the mouths of mountain streams. During the seasonal spates areas of water-logged silt *(limans)* were formed, and in these the grain was sown. At a later stage the flow of water was regulated by means of dykes or dams; and later still came the digging of irrigation canals.

In 1949-50 the upper levels of Namazga-Depe were excavated by B.A. Litvinsky. The excavations yielded large quantities of material, in particular decorated pottery, and revealed the layout of a large building.

In 1952 Namazga-Depe and a number of other sites were studied by the well-known expert on the Bronze Age in Transcaucasia, B.A. Kuftin, who proposed a classification of the successive stages of development of the culture of the Eneolithic period and Bronze Age. This classification, Namazga I to VI, is now accepted by archaeologists as the standard time scale for these periods.

Results of outstanding importance were obtained from excavations at two other sites, Kara-Depe and Geoksyur, which represented the climax of the prehistoric agricultural civilisation of southern Turkmenia.

Excavation at Kara-Depe, a hill near the railway station of Artyk, not far from Ashkhabad, was begun in 1952 by B.A. Kuftin. After his tragic death in 1953 the work was carried on by V.M. Masson, I.N. Khlopin and V.I. Sarianidi. The excavations continued for several years, and showed that the hill of Kara-Depe had been occupied by a large and flourishing settlement, covering an area of some 37 acres, which continued in existence from the 4th to the middle of the 3rd millennium B.C. — i.e., from the Eneolithic to the full tide of the Bronze Age.

The same archaeologists studied the similar site of Geoksyur[4], 12 miles from the town of Tedzhen and some 60 miles from Kara-Depe. Taken together, the two sites yielded a wealth of material which enabled the excavators to build up a graphic and comprehensive picture of the development of culture during this period, and to define the place of southern Turkmenia among those civilisations of the ancient East which are often grouped together as the painted pottery cultures.

General

It is not the object of this study to give a detailed account of all the results obtained from the excavation of these sites, but they may be briefly summarised. In this period agriculture and stock-rearing became the basis of the economy. Agriculture depended on a skilfully regulated system of artificial irrigation, involving the digging of an extensive network of water channels, and stock-rearing developed considerably. The stock included large numbers of cattle, along with smaller animals. Metal came into general use, being employed in the manufacture of tools and implements, weapons, ornaments, etc. In the final phases of the Bronze Age the techniques of metalworking made great strides.

Human settlements now increased considerably in size. Well-made rectilinear adobe bricks, manufactured from clay with an admixture of straw, became the main building material. Houses containing many rooms were built, on a more elaborate plan, with rooms designed for various different functions. The settlements were laid out with some degree of regularity, the houses being arranged in groups which were separated by streets, and were surrounded by walls of beaten mud — the first beginnings of defensive ramparts.

The most colourful material of this period is the very fine painted pottery. Its beginnings have already been noted at Dzheytun. In its later stages the decoration becomes more elaborate, both in pattern and colouring. The best specimens of this pottery achieve real artistic quality.

The specialists have distinguished a succession of different styles of decorated pottery (*Plates 8-17, 21*). The monochrome pottery shows a variety of geometric patterns, but figures of wild animals are also frequently found *(Plates 15, 16)*. The polychrome pottery is represented by vessels decorated with geometric designs which are remarkable both for their tonal range and their accomplished draughtsmanship. It is noteworthy that the design is applied freehand, without the use of stencils or patterns. At the same time the technical skill of the potters shows a marked advance. Kilns had now been developed in which firing was carried out at a temperature of up to 1200° C.

The arts are also represented by sculpture and by pottery figurines of animals, which in spite of their primitive quality are of remarkable expressiveness *(Plates 2, 3, 5, 6)*.

All the material recovered in the excavations goes to show that these communities were able to accumulate a surplus of products, which stimulated the development of trade and, as a consequence, led to increased cultural exchanges between different parts of the Near East, even between areas at a considerable distance from one another.

There is much data pointing to an increased rate of population growth, and this in turn led to the first indications of migratory movements.

The high standards achieved by the civilisation of the Bronze Age are particularly evident in the stage of development revealed in the upper levels at Namazga-Depe (Namazga IV and V), which are dated between 2400 and 1700 B.C.

This stage saw further progress in farming and stock-rearing. The techniques of artificial irrigation improved considerably, and this period also seems to have seen the appearance of the plough and of two- and four-wheeled vehicles. To this period, too, belong the invention of the potter's wheel and an important advance in firing technique, the two-level kiln. The pottery produced shows clear evidence of the professionalisation of production, with a marked tendency towards mass production and a consequent simplification and standardisation of the product. The splendid painted pottery gradually falls out of use and is replaced by other types of ware, made from stone or metal. A study of the layout of the settlement shows that the different trades were already grouped in their own separate districts.

The same process of professionalisation is found in metalworking, weaving and other forms of production. Among the objects found on sites belonging to Namazga-Depe IV and V the pottery and stone seals are of particular interest. They point to the development of private property and an unequal distribution of wealth, and this is confirmed by another significant observation: certain tombs are now found to contain considerable quantities of grave goods, a practice unknown in earlier periods.

All these processes reflect significant changes in the social structure, in which we can clearly trace the beginnings of a social differentiation of society.

It must, however, be observed that the developments we have been discussing, as a number of special studies (Gordon Childe, V.M. Masson) show, did not by any means proceed at the same pace throughout the whole of the

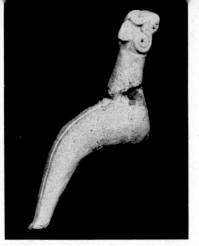
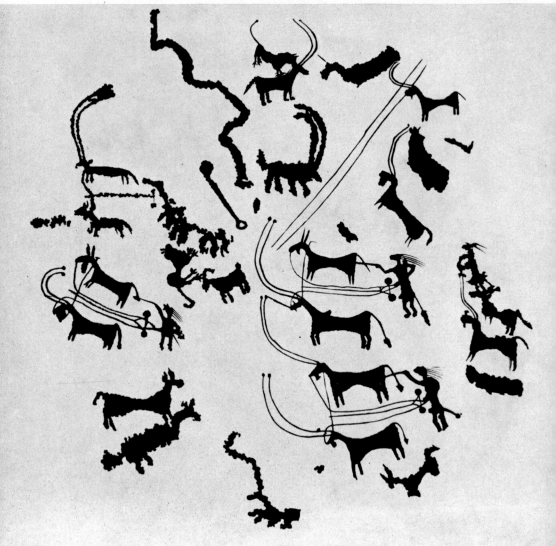

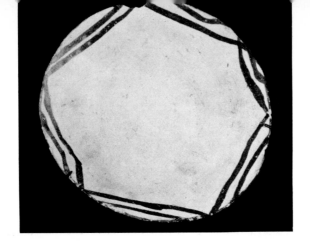

8, 9

12, 13

14

15, 16

18, 19   20-22 →

Near East. In some areas the evolution took place very rapidly, leading to the emergence of a new urban civilisation — Childe's "urban revolution", marked by the appearance of towns in southern Mesopotamia, India and Egypt. With the rise of the towns the unevenness of development became still more marked, both in the cultural and in the social and economic fields. In the urban civilisations the art of writing appears, and we learn from the written sources of the earliest forms of state organisation.

Southern Turkmenia was certainly on the threshold of this stage, but here the rise of urban civilisation and the development of state organisation took place at a much later date.

Other Civilisations of the Neolithic and the Bronze Age

In the last thirty years archaeologists have been active in other parts of Central Asia as well. Their work has shown that the conditions in which the Neolithic and Bronze Age cultures were formed in these areas were very different from those of southern Turkmenia, and that in consequence the general character of these cultures was also substantially different.

The Cultures of Khorezm

The Neolithic culture of Khorezm is known as the Kelteminar culture, a term introduced by S.P. Tolstov, from the name of a village near the site. The name of the site itself, however—the first Neolithic occupation site to be investigated in Khorezm—is Dzhanbas-Kala 4. The animal remains found here show that the main occupations of the inhabitants were hunting and fishing. They lived in large huts with an area of some 3,200 square feet, roofed with rushes, each of which could accommodate a large family unit of over 100 people. The very varied material found on the site included implements of stone (flint) and bone, and fragments of round-bottomed pottery vessels with stamped and incised decoration.

The characteristic Bronze Age culture is the Tazabagyab culture, which is found on many sites. The most informative Bronze Age site in Khorezm is the occupation site known as Kokcha III, where a tomb was excavated which yielded interesting anthropological and cultural material. The dead were buried in a flexed position in pits dug in the ground. They were frequently buried in couples, a man and a woman lying face to face. Various grave goods were buried along with the dead. The pottery consisted mainly of cooking pots decorated with simple patterns, usually incised, in the form of straight or zigzag lines or simple geometric figures (triangles). The bronze articles included awls, pendants, bracelets and other ornaments.

The inhabitants of this settlement lived in semi-subterranean huts with roofs borne on posts. Their main occupations were farming, based on artificial irrigation, and stock-rearing (cattle, horses and the smaller domestic animals).

The Hissar Culture

This name is given to a Neolithic culture which is widely distributed in the mountain areas of southern Tadzhikistan. Most of the sites so far known were excavated by V.A. Ranov. The material found here is entirely of stone (mainly a grey conglomerate, with a small amount of flint). The dwellings are difficult to locate. On some sites areas of flooring have been discovered, laid with a mixture of plaster and ashes, with the bases of large pots set into the ground. The main occupation of the inhabitants was hunting, but traces of a primitive form of agriculture were also found.

Related cultures, resembling the Hissar culture in many respects, have also been found in the north-eastern parts of Central Asia, reaching as far as the Semirechye.

The Kayrakkum Culture

Many sites belonging to this culture have been found on the left bank of the Syr-Darya, on the western boundaries of Ferghana. The culture was investigated in 1955-56 by B.A. Litvinsky, A.P. Okladnikov and V.A. Ranov. Of the dwellings themselves only a few traces could be identified, but a large quantity of interesting and significant material was found. In some cases the settlements occupied a very large area—up to 25 acres—but most of them ranged between a quarter of an acre and 7½ acres. The dimensions of the houses could be determined from the position of the hearths; they reached a length of 65 feet, with a width of 50 feet. The inhabitants lived by farming and stock-rearing, but hunting and fishing also played a part in their economy.

Their domestic animals included cattle, sheep and horses. That they grew grain is shown by the large number of querns which were found. The remarkably fine casting moulds and the bronze articles which were also found provided evidence of the high standard of development of the local bronze-working techniques, favoured by the proximity of deposits of copper ore. Evidently a considerable proportion of the population was engaged in mining, and the manufactured articles produced here provided an object of exchange.

Some extremely interesting pottery was found here, often moulded round a cloth bag filled with sand, traces of which were left on the inner surface of the vessels. The pottery was decorated in various ways — with a serrated stamp or with incised linear patterns.

The tombs discovered in the Kayrakkum area showed that the dead were buried in trenches lined with stone slabs.

The Chust Culture

The Ferghana valley has been intensively studied by archaeologists in the last thirty years, and is now one of the best known areas in Central Asia, particularly as regards the prehistoric period. The foundations of the study of Bronze Age culture in Ferghana were laid by B.A. Latynin in the 1930s, and a number of archaeologists are at present working in this area.

Of the Bronze Age sites discovered here the large settlement named after the village of Chust is of particular interest. It was discovered by E. Voronets and is being excavated by I.V. Sprishevsky. Another settlement at Dalverzin belonging to the same culture is being investigated by Y.A. Zadneprovsky. The former has an area of some 20 acres, the latter some 50 acres.

The settlement of Dalverzin already possessed a powerful defensive wall, partly constructed of adobe bricks. The houses were built on ground level, but their layout has not been fully established.

That farming was the main occupation of the inhabitants is shown by the finding of seeds of cultivated plants and of various implements, particularly sickles. Stock-rearing played a considerable part in the economy: the excavators found bones of cattle, sheep and goats, horses, pigs, asses and dogs.

Tools and implements were made of bronze, stone (sickles) and bone. Many objects associated with weaving were found.

The pottery of Chust is of great interest, showing a remarkable variety of form. In addition to ordinary domestic ware, it includes some magnificent thin-walled table ware. This was covered with a red slip and after glazing was decorated with a pattern in black, usually in the form of cross-hatched triangles but sometimes in scrolls and volutes.

The Zaman-Baba Culture

In recent years a Bronze Age culture has been discovered by Y.G. Gulyamov in the lower Zeravshan valley, in the western part of the Kyzyl-Kum desert.

It is known as the Zaman-Baba culture, after the name of the site where it was found. This culture is represented by the remains of dwellings (semi-subterranean huts), tombs and a variety of objects showing that the population was engaged in farming and stock-rearing. The pottery is of great interest; the decoration is incised or stamped, or sometimes painted.

Conclusions

This brief account of sites in Central Asia belonging to the Neolithic period and the Bronze Age — the time when a settled civilisation of farmers and stock-rearers grew up — is very far from being a complete list of all the sites now known. Archaeologists working in Central Asia, in addition to publishing their results, have done a great deal of work in interpreting them and drawing conclusions from them. The main questions with they they have been concerned are the dating of particular sites and the determination of relationships not only between the various sites within Central Asia itself but also with similar cultures beyond its boundaries. Some of these problems have not been easy to solve, and many dates assigned in the early stages of investigation have had to be reviewed. In this process help can frequently be obtained from radiocarbon dating.

It is now fairly well established that the chronological development of the settled farming cultures did not proceed at the same pace throughout Central Asia. Although the cultures of the south-western area (southern Turkmenia) reached their peak in the 4th-3rd millennium B.C., the climax of the other cultures which developed in the north-eastern part of Central Asia is to be dated at least a millennium later, and in some cases the rate of development was even slower. The cultures of these two areas also differed considerably in character.

Corresponding differences are found in the external relationships of the cultures in these two areas. In general, the cultures of the south-western area looked to the ancient centres of civilisation in Iran and Mesopotamia, while the lines of communication of the north-eastern area ran northward towards the great belt of steppe which stretches from the lower Volga to the eastern boundaries of Kazakhstan. In this area developed the Bronze Age culture known as the Andronovo culture, which reached its peak in the 2nd millennium B.C.

The characteristics of the Chust pottery suggested to the experts who studied it that this culture was connected with the Yang Shao civilisation which developed in eastern Turkestan and the Far East.

The end of the period which we have been discussing is marked by a distinct drawing together of the cultures of the two areas, which can be seen on sites lying on the boundary between the two areas — for example, in the upper levels at Anau or, even more strikingly, at Zaman-Baba. The excavations at Anau yielded pottery with the incised ornament found throughout almost the whole of the north-eastern area, and the painted pottery of Zaman-Baba undoubtedly reveals the influence of the cultures of the south-western area. The same type of pottery is found in Khorezm. This process of assimilation between the different cultures of Central Asia which can be observed at the end of the Bronze Age continues with increased intensity in the following period, when iron comes into general use and we pass from prehistory into history — the Iron Age.

CENTRAL ASIA IN THE EARLY HISTORICAL PERIODS

The Achaemenid Period

The first historical information about Central Asia and its peoples is contained in Herodotus, who had access to a number of written sources but obtained most of his information in the course of his journeyings through western Asia. In general Herodotus's information, which relates to the 5th century B.C., is reasonably reliable.

The Ancient Sources

There exists a still older source, the *Avesta*. This sacred book of the Zoroastrians is a highly complex work, and there has been much dispute among scholars about the place and time of composition of its various parts. It is now fairly generally accepted, however, that Zoroaster himself, the prophet or the reformer of the religion which bears his name (Zoroastrianism), lived in the 6th century B.C. and was a native of Bactria, where he began his proselytising activity.

The most important written sources on the early history of the peoples of Central Asia are the various inscriptions by the Achaemenid kings on rock faces and buildings, and in particular the famous Behistun inscription (520 B.C.), often called "the queen of inscriptions".

One other early source may be mentioned — the memoirs of Ctesias, a Greek doctor at the court of the Achaemenid King Artaxerxes II (405-359), which have survived only in fragments. The value of Ctesias' work was for long under-estimated; in particular he suffered from comparison with Herodotus, and was even dismissed as a liar and a fabricator. Not until the 20th century was he appreciated at his true worth. The credit for his rehabilitation belongs to two outstanding scholars who were active in the early part of the century, J. Marquart and V.V. Bartold. In Marquart's view, Ctesias' work incorporated "fragments of an ancient Iranian heroic epic"; and Bartold demonstrated convincingly that his stories were "permeated with Bactro-Sacian influences" and were closely related to themes found many centuries later in Firdausi's famous poem, the *Shahnama*, the heroic element in which he suggested was of "eastern Iranian origin"[5].

The information contained in these sources about the peoples of Central Asia has been absorbed into the accepted body of knowledge and need not be reproduced here. A few general points may, however, be noted.

All these sources confirm and complement one another in giving the first account of the principal regions of Central Asia and the races who inhabited them. To a considerable extent the geographical and ethnic names they record remained in use for many centuries. Thus in addition to Bactria, which occupied an extensive area on both sides of the upper and middle Amu-Darya, now part of southern Central Asia and northern Afghanistan, we find mention in the sources of Margiana, Parthyene (corresponding to present-day southern Turkmenia and part of Khurasan in north-eastern Iran), Khorezm (on the lower Amu-Darya), and Sogd or Sogdiana (the valley of the River Zeravshan).

These regions were inhabited mainly by settled farming peoples, who are known by the names of the areas they occupied. To them must no doubt be added the Paricani, a tribe whose name is to be identified with Ferghana. Our information about this area, however, is extremely uncertain.

The sources have much to say about nomadic tribes like the Massagetae and the Sacae or Sacians, both of whom are described as Scythian peoples. About the Sacae, for example, Herodotus makes the interesting remark: "These Sacae, or Scyths... were in truth Amyrgian Scythians, but the Persians called them Sacae, since that is the name which they give to all Scythians."[6] The Massagetae occupied an area round the Aral Sea; the territory of the Sacae lay to the east of the Amu-Darya basin and included the steppe areas of Kazakhstan.

The principal rivers of Central Asia, the Amu-Darya and the Syr-Darya, appear in the Greek sources under the names of the Oxus and the Jaxartes, the latter being confused with the River Don.

The Historical Data

Cyrus (550-530), the founder of the Achaemenid empire, apparently undertook a number of campaigns in Central Asia; and the fact that several campaigns were required is an indication of the stubborn resistance which he encountered. The king himself was killed in a war against the Massagetae. The Behistun inscription tells us of a great rising against Darius I in Margiana in 522 B.C., led by one Frada of Margiana. The scale of the rising is shown by the numbers killed and taken prisoner, which are precisely recorded as 55,243 killed and 6,572 prisoners. The people of Parthyene and the Sacae likewise rebelled against Darius (521-518 B.C.); and the name and likeness of the leader of the Sacae, Skunkha, are immortalised on the cliff at Behistun.

Beyond these facts we have not much information about the two centuries of Achaemenid rule in Central Asia; but what we do know points to the great influence which the Achaemenids had on many aspects of the life of the people. The administrative organisation of the Persian Empire, for example, was extended to Central Asia, the various regions being included in satrapies which also took in the neighbouring areas. Herodotus records the very substantial sums which these satrapies were required to pay by way of annual tributes into the treasury of the "Great Kings", and Central Asia provided gold and the much prized lapis lazuli for the adornment of the splendid buildings erected by the Achaemenids in their capitals at Persepolis and Susa.

We learn at the same time that the Central Asian tribes — the Bactrians, the Sacae, the Chorasmians and others — supplied men for military units which operated in the distant western parts of the Empire and took part in campaigns against Egypt and Greece. From later sources which relate the history of Alexander's campaigns we learn also that there was in Central Asia at this period at least one large colony of Greeks from the coastal area of Asia Minor. The same sources tell us that by the time of Alexander's campaigns there had developed a powerful local aristocracy, probably based on the ownership of land, which was enrolled in the administrative organisation of the Achaemenid state. It is evident that in these circumstances there must have been an intensive cultural interchange between Central Asia and the other parts of the Empire, particularly the western regions, and that consequently there must have been some degree of assimilation and unification of different cultures, especially among the dominant classes of the population.

The Oxus Treasure

We can gain some idea of the culture of the Achaemenid period from the collection of objects found in Central Asia in the late seventies of last century — the hoard known as the Amu-Darya Treasure or Oxus Treasure, now in the British Museum. From the archaeological point of view it is regrettable that nothing is known of the circumstances in which this magnificent hoard was found. We cannot be certain that all the objects were found in the same place, nor that the present collection includes everything that originally belonged to it. Nor is the collection homogeneous in terms of date: most of the objects can be certainly dated to the time of the Achaemenid Empire, but some of them are later. It is, however, reliably established that the treasure was found in southern Tadzhikistan, near Kobadian (now Mikoyanabad).

The Archaeology of Urban Sites

Less spectacular, but more informative about the local culture of this period, is the material produced by the most recent excavations — though it is still not sufficient to enable us to paint a complete picture of the life of the people.

The most important fact established by these investigations is the development of urban life, evidenced by the emergence of large urban centres in Central Asia in the Achaemenid period.

Urban settlements of varying size dating from the 6th to the 4th century B.C. are known in all the principal regions of Central Asia. We need refer only to one or two of the most important. In southern Turkmenia there was the ancient city of Gyaur-Kala (Merv), with a circumference of more than 4 miles, and in Khorezm there were the large towns of Kalaly-Gir and Kyuzeli-Gir. The latter, following the configuration of the hill on which it was built, was triangular in shape, with a length of 1,100 yards and a greatest width of over 550 yards, and was surrounded by a double ring of defensive walls with towers. The town of Kalaly-Gir was of similar type.

The chief town of Sogdiana at this period was Marakanda (Afrosiab). According to the account given by the Roman historian Quintus Curtius Rufus — though this is probably exaggerated — the walls of this city had a circuit of 70 stadia, or more than 6 miles. In southern Tadzhikistan, the site of Kala-i-Mir represents the remains of a settlement of the 6th to 4th centuries. The capital of Bactria was the town of the same name, Bactra, the remains of which at Bala-Hissar date from the Achaemenid period and occupy an area of almost 300 acres. To this period also belongs the large site of Shurabashat in eastern Ferghana. Unfortunately the Achaemenid levels at these sites often lie at a considerable depth and are consequently difficult to excavate; but in spite of this the archaeologists have been able to recover a good deal of interesting material.

The excavations at Kyuzeli-Gir in Khorezm, for example, show a considerable advance in architectural technique. Here a large building containing many rooms was excavated, along with associated buildings in which the bases of columns were found: evidently the builders had now learned how to carry their roofs on columns, a method previously unknown in

Central Asia. The adobe bricks which were the principal building material were now made in standard sizes. Iron had come into general use. The material found in greatest quantity, however, was wheel-turned pottery *(Plates 18-20):* this was evidently now a highly developed craft industry. A significant feature in this respect is the standardisation and uniformity of design of pottery in all the main regions of Central Asia. Everywhere we find well-made vessels of cylindrical or cylindro-conical shape with a pedestal base, usually decorated with a brightly coloured slip *(Plate 18)*. Vessels of these shapes have been found in Achaemenid levels beyond the bounds of Central Asia, on such sites as Balkh and Nad-i-Ali in Afghanistan.

In addition to studying the towns themselves, archaeologists have also devoted much attention to such important features of economic life in Central Asia as the irrigation systems, which made considerable progress in this period, with the construction of large canals, dams and other works.

Sacian Tombs

Material of great interest has been recovered from tombs constructed by nomadic tribes — for the most part undoubtedly Sacae — in the 6th to 4th centuries B.C., which have been found in some of the peripheral areas of north-eastern Central Asia. Recently particular interest has been aroused by the discovery of Sacian tombs in the delta of the Syr-Darya (the Tegiskan and Uygarak cemeteries) and on many other sites in the central Tien Shan and the Pamirs.

The tombs of the Sacae living in the Syr-Darya area are contained in earth mounds *(kurgans)* of varying heights. The dead were buried in pits up to 6 feet deep, lying on a bed of grass and rushes and covered with matting and timber. In some cases the practice of cremation is found. The tombs had been robbed, and all that remained for the excavators was a few scattered objects, though these were very typical of the whole. They included some fine pieces of pottery, bronze arrowheads, the upper part

of an iron sword, gold plates from a belt, and pieces of bronze harness —
in particular a characteristic type of bit and some splendidly made buckles
in the "animal style" with heads of a mountain sheep and a griffin.

The excavation of Sacian tombs in the Tien Shan and the Pamirs (by
A.N. Bernshtam and B.A. Litvinsky) yielded an even larger quantity of
material, including many objects designed either for use or for ornament.

The burial practice in these tombs was rather different. The graves were
shallow pits, and the dead were buried in a flexed position and sprinkled
with red ochre. The tombs were covered with low mounds of stone or
earth, surrounded by circles of stone slabs. Many of the tombs were
"cenotaphs" — i.e., they contained no burials: no doubt these tombs had
been erected in honour of some dead warrior who had fallen far from his
family burial place. The grave goods included a remarkable variety of
objects — pottery and weapons, including the Scythian short sword *(akinakes)*, battle-axes, and arrows with heads of bronze, iron or bone. Many
metal harness ornaments with figures of animals were also found. Certain
individual items are of particular interest: for example a bronze pot with
the head of a griffin, and an iron dagger with a bronze haft, decorated
with the heads of mountain sheep and ending in a full-length figure of a
mountain sheep *(Plate 22)*.

The works of art and craftsmanship found in the Sacian tombs demonstrate
the affinities of Sacian culture with the wider Scythian world, on the one
hand, and with the culture of the settled areas of Central Asia on the other —
in particular with the material contained in the Oxus Treasure.

The Greek Period

In three great battles Alexander of Macedon crushed the military power
of the Achaemenid empire and gained possession of its western territories

and its capital of Persepolis. The attempts of the last Achaemenid king, Darius III, to collect new forces in the eastern parts of the empire to carry on the war against his Macedonian adversary ended tragically when he was treacherously killed by Bessus, satrap of Bactria, who had declared himself heir to the Achaemenid dynasty. Bessus in turn, however, met the same fate. We have no evidence of any activity by the mass of the people in support of the fallen dynasty, either in the conquered western areas or in Iran itself.

Alexander's Conquest

Against this background the stubborn resistance with which the peoples of Central Asia met Alexander, lasting three years (329-327 B.C.) is a fact of undoubted significance. But it was not inspired by support for the defeated Achaemenids: it was directed against the new conquerors. Like all Alexander's campaigns, these three bloody years have been thoroughly studied by scholars, and it is unnecessary to give any account of the course of the war. We may note, however, that Alexander's campaign strained his resources to the utmost and involved him in heavy losses.

Alexander undoubtedly learnt a number of lessons from his war with the peoples of Central Asia. This is shown by his establishment of a large number of strong points and fortresses throughout Central Asia, and also by his persistent efforts to win over the local aristocracy. Henceforth the foundations of Alexander's policy in the conquered territories were the establishment of close relations with the aristocratic elements in local society and the building of towns and fortified settlements for Macedonian garrisons.

Until quite recently it was fairly generally accepted by historians that the building of towns in Central Asia dated from the time of Alexander. The example usually quoted was Alexandria Eschate ("Farthest Alexandria"), which is identified with the modern town of Khodzhent (now Leninabad).

At the end of the 1930s this point of view was given expression by W.W. Tarn in these words: "Alexander had now reached a part of the world where towns were almost unknown... If Alexander wanted cities in eastern Iran he must build them."[7]

The erroneousness of this view is now evident. Archaeological investigation has shown that many towns and fortified settlements were established long before Alexander's campaigns; and the written sources recording his military operations contain quite unambiguous references to the existence of a number of towns. Nevertheless it is clear that the period of Alexander and his successors was a time of active town building. In this respect Central Asia is not very different from the countries of the western Hellenistic world, with their strongly marked urban character. It must be added, however, that the ancient historians had, if anything, a rather exaggerated idea of the degree of urbanisation of Central Asia and the neighbouring regions in the Hellenistic period.

In the most general terms the history of Central Asia in this period can be summarised as follows. Apart from the ten years of rule by the Diadochi (323-312 B.C.), Central Asia formed part of the Seleucid empire until the middle of the 3rd century B.C., being governed by viceroys who also bore the title of satraps, as under the Achaemenids. In the middle of the 3rd century, however, the situation in the eastern parts of the Seleucid possessions changed radically, when the Indian territories conquered by Alexander fell away and an independent Parthian kingdom was formed in north-eastern Iran. The satrap of Bactria thereupon also declared his independence, establishing a state which is known to historians as the Greco-Bactrian kingdom. In this kingdom were included the principal regions of Central Asia.

The Greco-Bactrian Kingdom

There is still controversy about the boundaries of the kingdom, particularly about its northern limits. The most extreme view would put the north-eastern boundary of the Greco-Bactrian kingdom at the height of its power on the very borders of China; but this view rests only on a passing remark in one of the sources.

On the evidence of the find-spots of the famous Greco-Bactrian coins — although this is not, of course, conclusive — the Greco-Bactrian kingdom included northern Bactria (the southern part of present-day Uzbekistan and Tadzhikistan) and the whole of Sogdiana as far as the Tashkent region. Margiana was an object of contention between Greco-Bactria and the Parthian kingdom, and about the middle of the 2nd century B.C. was incorporated in the latter. It is still uncertain whether such areas as Ferghana and Khorezm were under the control of the Greco-Bactrian kingdom, although coins issued by the Greek kings are found here too. Some Soviet historians believe that alongside the Greco-Bactrian and Parthian kingdoms there flourished in northern Central Asia the kingdom of the K'ang-kiu, centred on Khorezm. This has not, however, been generally accepted.

However this may be, the political hegemony of the Greeks in Central Asia lasted until the thirties of the 2nd century B.C. The Parthian kingdom had a much longer life than the Greco-Bactrian kingdom, surviving into the 3rd century A.D. in control of south-western Central Asia.

The two centuries of Greek rule in Central Asia (from Alexander's arrival in 329 B.C. to the fall of the Greco-Bactrian kingdom about 130 B.C.) have attracted much attention from western European historians. The results of many studies of particular questions and a number of general studies of the Greco-Bactrian kingdom are brought together in Sir William Tarn's well-known work, *The Greeks in Bactria and India* (first edition 1938, second edition 1951, reprinted 1966). Although many of its conclusions are open to question, this work gives an excellent comprehensive account of the culture of Central Asia in this period. Leaving aside the political situation — which in any event is confused and in many respects obscure —

23, 24

26, 27

← 28   29, 30

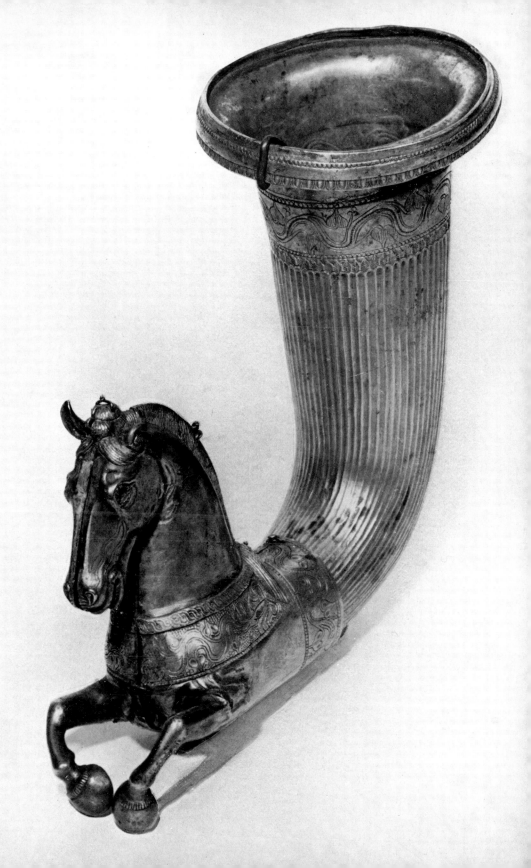

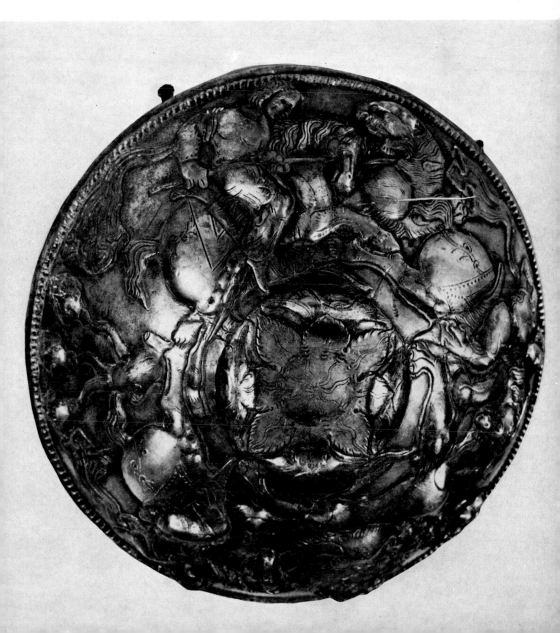

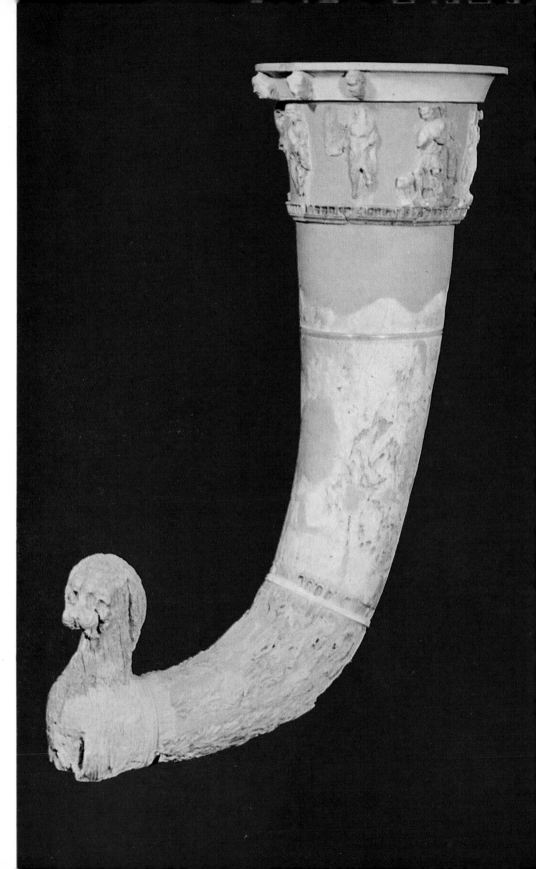

it is fair to say that the ancient authors who wrote about Central Asia as it was in this period painted a reasonably accurate picture of the natural conditions of Central Asia and certain features of its economy. While noting that a large part of the country was desert, they nevertheless refer to the high fertility of the soil, the generally high standard of agriculture and the development of artificial irrigation. In some cases the information they give is grossly exaggerated: Pliny talks, for example, of a strain of wheat cultivated in Central Asia with grains as large as a normal ear, and of bunches of grapes a cubit long.

In these ancient accounts much stress is laid on the development of urban life, indicated by the frequent reference to the Greco-Bactrian kingdom as the "land of a thousand cities". Without taking references of this kind at their face value as exact factual statements, we can accept them as reflecting the reality of a high level of development of agriculture and an upsurge of town building.

Our most important evidence on the culture of this period is provided by the coins of the Greco-Bactrian kings, which have come down to us in considerable numbers. The silver coins of various denominations are of remarkable artistic quality — accepted masterpieces of the metalworker's craft.

In 1940 the Soviet scholar Kamila Trever published her study, *Monuments of Greco-Bactrian Art*, in which not only the coins but a variety of works of art (in particular works of toreutic art) in museums throughout the world were discussed for the first time as examples of Greco-Bactrian art. In the overwhelming majority of cases these objects were identified as Greco-Bactrian on the basis of stylistic analysis. For many items the place of finding was not known; and even when it was this gave little clue to the place of manufacture. In these circumstances it is not surprising that the reference of some of them to the Greco-Bactrian period is disputed. The majority of the attributions, however, are clearly correct; and the result of this analysis of works of art has been to produce a fuller picture of a number of important aspects of Greco-Bactrian culture than can be obtained from the written sources.

Let us now turn to the specifically archaeological evidence, which has revealed the existence of many urban settlements in Central Asia which were either founded or continued to exist in this period.

Urban sites in Bactriana

With the help of ancient Buddhist texts it has now been shown that the present-day name of the town of *Termez* is a distortion of the name of its founder, the Greco-Bactrian king Demetrius. That Termez was founded in the Greco-Bactrian period is confirmed by the finding on this site of many Greco-Bactrian coins and other objects dated to the same period. These include in particular some stone column bases, typical of Greek work of this period, found on the town site and in the immediate neighbourhood. Greco-Bactrian coins and other material belonging to this period have also been found in many other areas round Termez.

Unfortunately, however, the excavation of the levels belonging to this period presents difficulty because they lie buried at a considerable depth under later levels. The excavators have therefore had to confine themselves to digging small trial shafts, which have given a comparatively poor yield of material (fragments of pottery). Of more interest are the finds of terracotta figures of men and animals dating from this period.

The site of *Key-Kobad-Shakh*, discovered in 1949 by M.M. Dyakonov a mile from Kobadian on the right bank of the River Kafirnigan, was more accessible to excavation, which was carried out here over a relatively large area. It revealed the remains of a town occupying an area 420 yards by 310 yards in extent, surrounded by a defensive wall built of rectangular bricks. An interesting feature of the bricks is the occurrence on them of a variety of symbols, including many letters of the Greek alphabet. The wall was reinforced with rectangular towers at regular intervals. The walls ran in an absolutely straight line, and in the middle of each side was a gate. The principal streets, leading from one gate to another and crossing in the middle at right angles, divided the town into separate districts of regular shape. A partial excavation of the built-up area has shown that the town was laid out on a uniform plan. The large quantity of pottery and other objects recovered in the excavations indicates a high level of craft production *(Plate 39)*.

In 1953-54 a small site, covering an area 270 yards by 140 yards, was excavated on the left bank of the River Vakhsh, some distance above its junction with the Amu-Darya, at *Kukhn-Kala*. This also, shows a regular plan, but according to its discoverer, B.A. Litvinsky, seems to have remained unfinished.

On the basis of exploratory excavations a number of other towns are also assigned to the Greco-Bactrian period. In the valley of the River Surkhan-Darya, for example, there are the site of Khayrabad-Tepe and the large town site of Dalverzin-Tepe, near Denau. At the village of Shakhrinau, near Dushanbe, the capital of Tadzhikistan, a town site with an area of some 860 acres has been discovered. All these sites, however, still await investigation.

In recent years some very promising discoveries have been made in southern Bactria, in what is now Afghanistan. Material of sensational interest has been found by the French expedition which has been excavating the site of Ai-Hanum, on the banks of the Amu-Darya. Externally this site is very similar to the Central Asian sites. The uppermost levels yielded material belonging to the Greco-Bactrian period, including Greek inscriptions, works of art, and architectural details and structural features (tiles, antefixes, metopes, capitals, etc.). Ai-Hanum, being conveniently accessible for large-scale excavations, is clearly destined to be a key site in the archaeology of the Greco-Bactrian period.[8]

Other Urban Sites

In addition to the sites within Bactria itself, a number of interesting sites, either wholly of the Greco-Bactrian period or having well-defined levels belonging to this period, have been investigated in Sogdiana, Khorezm and southern Turkmenia.

Important material on the culture of the Greco-Bactrian period has been found at *Afrosiab* in the two levels known as Afrosiab II and III. In the opinion of the excavator, A.I. Terenozhkin, pottery production reached its highest development in Afrosiab III. The pottery in this level, he says, "is remarkable for the purity of the clay, the fineness and density of its texture, and its elegance of form *(Plates 40, 42)*. The smaller vessels are decorated not only with a red slip of excellent quality but with a red glaze."[9] Terenozhkin notes also that baked bricks appear for the first time in this period.

In the circumstances in which excavation was carried out on this site it was not possible to study other types of material, in particular the architecture.

Of the sites in Khorezm belonging to the Hellenistic period the first to be mentioned is *Dzhanbas-Kala*. On this site the defensive walls were well preserved, and investigation showed that the system of fortification used in Khorezm in this period differed significantly from the Bactrian system. The town site, rectangular in plan, was surrounded by a double circuit of walls, forming a two-storey corridor from which the defenders could fire on the enemy. For this purpose the outer wall — which had no towers — was pierced by a system of loopholes, arranged alternately on the upper and the lower levels. The entrance, in the middle of the north wall, was strengthened by further elaborate defensive works. There was one principal street, which ran from the entrance to the opposite wall, dividing the town into two parts.

Another Hellenistic site in Khorezm is *Koy-Krylgan-Kala,* one of the few ancient sites in Central Asia which have been almost completely excavated. In spite of this the function of the site still remains mysterious. It is chiefly remarkable for its unusual circular plan (diameter 285 feet). The excavations have shown that during its lengthy period of occupation (from the 4th century B.C. to the 1st century A.D.) the layout of Koy-Krylgan-Kala underwent considerable alteration. Originally there was in the centre of the site a round two-storied building (diameter 140 feet), with rooms arranged on a regular plan; the rest of the area within the ramparts was an open courtyard. Later the courtyard was covered with other buildings, and the ramparts were reinforced by a new wall with nine towers. In S.P. Tolstov's opinion the central building was used for cult purposes.

The excavations at Koy-Krylgan-Kala yielded an extraordinary abundance of material, mainly pottery, which was remarkable for its great variety of form *(Plate 52).* Of particular interest were a number of pottery rhytons decorated with protomes of horses and griffins, flasks with a variety of stamped decorative reliefs, a large number of figurines of human beings and animals, remains of a large piece of sculpture in full relief, and fragments of wall paintings.

Among the Hellenistic sites so far discovered *Nisa* occupies a place of prime importance. The site, lying 8 miles from Ashkhabad near the village of Bagir, was first investigated in the 1930s by A.A. Marushchenko. Systematic excavation began in 1946 and was continued for several years by the Southern Turkmenian Archaeological Expedition under the direction of M.E. Masson.

There are in fact two separate sites a short distance from one another, Old and New Nisa. The remains of the town are at New Nisa, which continued to exist until the Middle Ages. The excavators concluded that Old Nisa was a royal residence, a closed city containing the palaces, the temples and the tombs of the Parthian kings, which went out of use at the end of the Parthian period (beginning of 3rd century A.D.).

The original name of the town was Mihrdatkart. Its layout differed from that of the normal Hellenistic towns, being pentagonal in shape. The ramparts, built of *pakhsa* (beaten clay) faced externally with adobe bricks, were enormously thick (25–30 feet), and were reinforced by towers. The excavations have revealed the architectural structure of the palaces and temples, which are remarkable for their large size. Thus one of the buildings excavated, the "square room", measures 65 feet each way, and the "round room" has a diameter of 55 feet.

Particular interest also attaches to the dwelling houses which have been excavated. These have large store-rooms of various kinds, including special wine cellars. The wine was kept in very large pottery jars, known as *khums*, buried in the ground. A cemetery area lying within the town (New Nisa) was also excavated.

The whole complex of remains is of first-rate importance for the contribution it makes to the history of Central Asian architecture. It is also difficult to over-estimate the significance of the works of art found at Nisa, particularly the sculpture. This consists mainly of monumental clay statues of human figures of over life size; but Nisa also yielded the first marble sculpture found in Central Asia — some of it, unfortunately, broken into countless fragments. It has been possible to restore two pieces of sculpture almost in their entirety. One of them is a copy a well-known ancient work showing Aphrodite wringing out her hair; the other is of a woman wearing a long dress, which is modelled with great skill.

Many pieces of small sculpture were also found — terracotta reliefs, silver and bronze figurines of animals, and a collection of figured seals *(bullae)*.

A discovery of unique importance was a group of rhytons carved from ivory *(Plates 31, 35-37)*. They were very badly damaged, but by dint of painstaking and meticulous effort most of them — some forty in number — have now been restored. The pointed end of the rhytons are decorated with sculptured protomes of centaurs, winged horses, lions, griffins and other monstrous creatures. Round the broad upper ends are bands of ornaments in relief, representing scenes connected with the cult of Dionysus, figures of the gods and goddesses of Olympus, and other favourite themes of Hellenistic art. Finally mention must be made of the finding of some 2,500 inscribed sherds or ostraca. All the inscriptions are in the Parthian language, written in the Aramaic alphabet. They are mainly records of the delivery of wine from various districts to the royal wine cellar, with an exact indication of the dates (2nd-1st century B.C.). This enormous collection of original documents, which in terms of quantity has no equal in Oriental epigraphy, represents the earliest known occurrence of the use of writing in Central Asia. It is a source of exceptional value for the illumination of many aspects of the social, economic and cultural situation in Parthia in the Hellenistic period.

38–40

41–43

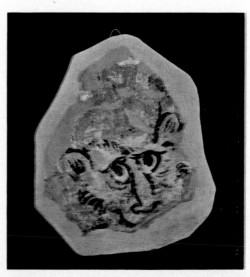

44–46

47–49

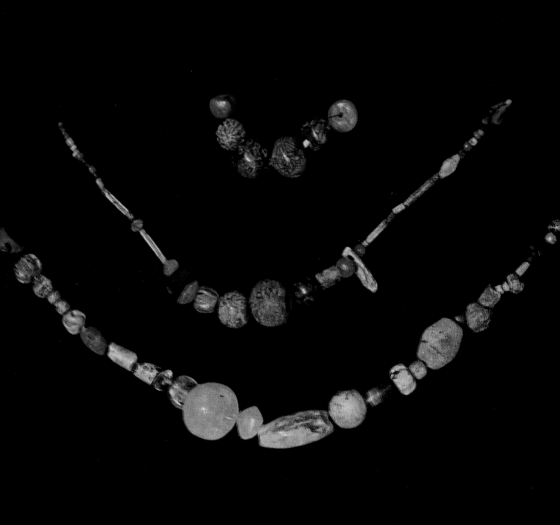

57, 58

59–61

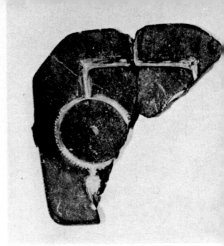

62–64

CENTRAL ASIA IN THE KUSHAN PERIOD

III

The Historical Framework

As we have seen, the Greco-Bactrian kingdom ceased to exist in the thirties of the 2nd century B.C. The fragmentary information which students of the period have managed to piece together shows that in spite of its brilliance and its military successes the Greco-Bactrian kingdom was internally unstable. The Greeks themselves, far from their homeland, represented only a negligible proportion of the total population of the territory they ruled. Moreover there were dissensions among them which led to frequent palace revolutions of extreme violence. Thus it is reported of Heliocles, who overthrew his father Eucratides, that he not only killed him but drove his chariot over the corpse. There is no doubt that the basic contradictions and the weakness of the kingdom lay in the hostility felt for the incomers by the great mass of the local population. The blow which led directly to the collapse of Greek dominance, however, was delivered by the warlike nomadic tribes which had made their way into Central Asia from the north-east. The appearance of these tribes was one episode in the great migration of nomadic peoples which was set in motion by the formation of the first "steppe empire" of the Huns. The Chinese chronicles give us a few basic dates for these events, together with the names of the tribes and their leaders, enabling us to build up some kind of picture of the situation.

The formation of the Hunnish empire was the achievement of their Shan-yu (leader) Mao-tun (206-165 B.C.). In the seventies of the 2nd century B.C. he defeated the tribes which had settled in certain parts of eastern Turkestan and Mongolia and are referred to in the Chinese sources as the Yueh-chi. The main body of these tribes (Ta Yueh-chi, the Great Yueh-chi) moved westward under pressure from the Huns, met with a hostile reception from the Wu-sun tribes in the foothills of the Tien Shan (Semirechye), and after defeating them came into conflict with the Sai tribes. In the Chinese name of this last group of tribes it is not difficult to recognise the Sacae, with

93

whom we are already familiar. Of the Sai tribes we are told that they were dispersed and that "the king of the Sai withdrew to the south". The Wu-sun, however, quickly recovered and, with the help of the Huns, not only compelled the Yueh-chi to leave their territory but even gained possession of "the former lands of the Sai". The Yueh-chi then made their way into Ferghana over the passes in the Tien Shan range and, we may suppose, were able, with the help of the local population, gradually to free almost the whole of Central Asia from Greek rule. About the detailed course of events in Central Asia we know nothing; but the final result is known to us from the report of the famous Chang-k'ien, an emissary of the Chinese Emperor Wu Ti who was sent on a special mission to the leaders of the Yueh-chi in 140 B.C. The object of the mission was to persuade the Yueh-chi to return to their former territory and make common cause against the Huns. Chang-k'ien took more than ten years — years full of adventures, including capture by the Huns — to reach the headquarters of the Yueh-chi. His quest ended in 128 B.C., when the Yueh-chi headquarters were on the northern bank of the Amu-Darya. His mission, however, was unsuccessful: for the Yueh-chi there could now be no question of leaving their new home on the Amu-Darya.

Literary and Epigraphical Sources

Chang-k'ien's account is a source of first-rate importance for the history of Central Asia. It contains a most valuable description of the territory between Ferghana and Bactria, and confirms the information from ancient western sources and from archaeology indicating that Central Asia in this period was a settled area with a flourishing agriculture and many towns. A point of significance to this study is that by the time Chang-k'ien reached the headquarters of the Yueh-chi Greek rule had already been swept away both north and south of the Amu-Darya, for he records that "Ta-hia (the name he gives to Bactria) has no supreme governor, each town being ruled by its own prince."[10]

The Chinese chronicles also contain much information about Central Asia. The *Hou-han-shu*, for example, gives a general summary of the political situation in the subsequent period, which is reproduced here with some abridgment: "When the house of the Yueh-chi was destroyed by the Huns it moved to Ta-hia and was divided into five princely houses — the Hsiu-mi, the Shuang-mi, the Kuei-shuang, the Hsi-tuen and the Tu-mi. After the passage of somewhat over a hundred years the Kuei-shuang prince Chi'u-chiu-ch'ueh overcame the other four princes and declared himself emperor under the title of ruler of the Kuei-shuang. He then went to war with An-si, conquered Kao-fu, destroyed Fu-tu and Chi-pin, and seized their territories. Chi'u-chiu-ch'ueh lived over eighty years. On his death his son Yen-kao-chen succeeded to the throne. He then conquered India, entrusting its government to one of his generals. From this time the Yueh-chi became a very wealthy and powerful house. The neighbouring states called it the kingdom of the Kuei-shuang, but the Chinese court continued to use the old name of the Great Yueh-chi."[11]

Quite clearly the form Kuei-shuang used in the chronicle represents the name Kushan; and on the basis of its rather loose dating ("somewhat over a hundred years") the first stage in the formation of the Kushan kingdom falls at the beginning of the Christian era.

These events did not pass unnoticed in the western sources, which on the whole are entirely consistent with the accounts just quoted. Thus Strabo, enumerating the nomadic tribes of Central Asia, writes: "Of these nomads the best known are those who captured Bactriana from the Greeks: that is, the Asii, the Pasiani, the Tochari and the Sacarauli, who came from the region on the other bank of the Jaxartes and from the region of the Sacae and the Sogdians, occupied by the Sacae."[12]

There has been much learned discussion about the identification of these tribes with the peoples referred to in the Chinese and other sources. There can be no doubt that Strabo is talking about the same tribes as are mentioned in the Chinese chronicle. The most interesting of the names he uses is that of the "Tochari". This name survived through the centuries and is attested right down to the 10th century in the geographical term of Tocharistan, applied in the Arab sources to the area on both sides of the Amu-Darya from the Hissar mountain range in the north to the Hindu Kush in the south: i.e., the former territory of Bactria. Some scholars think that it is possible to identify the Tochari with the tribes known to the Chinese as the "Ta-hia".

It is puzzling that such a well-informed writer as Strabo does not specifically mention the Kushans, although this name is attested in such objective evidence as the coins. It may be that they are concealed under such names as Asii or Pasiani, but of this we cannot be sure.

For the history of the Kushan kingdom — or, more correctly, of the Kushan dynasty — the most important source is provided by the coins of the Kushan kings, which invariably describe each ruler as a Kushan in addition to giving his name and royal style. The names of these kings were Heraos, Kujula Kadphises, Wima Kadphises, Kanishka I, Vasishka, Huvishka and Vasudeva. (Some students believe that the name of Kanishka was borne by two other kings. This is not, however, generally accepted, for the reigns of these seven kings, covering altogether some two centuries, comprehended the rise, the heyday and the decline of the kingdom).

In addition to the coins bearing the names of the Kushan kings we have also some epigraphic evidence in which the names of some of the Kushan kings are associated with particular dates.

In these circumstances it should apparently not be difficult to establish the chronology of the Kushan kingdom. And yet this question has given rise to an extensive literature and is one of the most controversial questions exercising contemporary historians. The difficulties are that the Kushan coins bear no date of issue and that the dated inscriptions give no indication of the era in which the dates are reckoned. Moreover some dates in inscriptions are expressed only as the regnal year of a particular king. As a result of this vagueness the dates assigned to the Kushan kingdom by different scholars vary within a range of almost 200 years. The dispute revolves round the date of accession of the best known Kushan king, Kanishka, the starting-point of the "Kanishka era". Some authorities put this at 78 A.D.; others, at the opposite extreme, bring it down to 278 A.D. Other scholars have suggested intermediate dates, for example 144 A.D. This situation creates serious difficulties for archaeological studies, since in practice the dating of excavations belonging to this period depends mainly on finds of Kushan coins.

Another unsolved problem which particularly concerns us in this study is the question of the northern frontier of the Kushan kingdom. We may, however, reasonably suppose that most of the territory between the Amu-Darya and the Syr-Darya was fairly firmly under Kushan control for the greater part of the period during which this dynasty was on the throne.

The Economic and Cultural Context

Before proceeding to discuss the archaeological sites in Central Asia belonging to the Kushan period I should like to note some of the main features of the economic and cultural life of Central Asia in the Kushan period, on the basis of the information provided by the written sources.

There is no doubt that the most important factor in the economic life of Central Asia in this period was the establishment under the Kushans of intensive trading relations between the Far East and the West, reaching as far as the eastern provinces of the Roman Empire. The main trade route was the "Great Silk Road", which gave Central Asia a vital rôle as an intermediate link in all international trade by the land route for many centuries. The activities of the Central Asian traders were not, of course, confined to the east-west route. There were also roads running north to the vast Eurasian steppes and south towards India. The development of urban life was closely associated with the growth of international trade, and the towns became centres of internal as well as international trade.

An event of outstanding importance during the Kushan period was the spread of Buddhism in Central Asia. The evidence suggests that this spread began in the reign of Kanishka I, who was well known as a patron of Buddhism. The enduring influence of Buddhism on the ideology and culture of the peoples of Central Asia needs no demonstration.

The Archaeological Evidence

Material of the Kushan period has been found on a very large number of excavated sites. Levels belonging to this period have been identified on all, or almost all, the town sites discussed earlier, and have been investigated at Samarkand (Afrosiab), Termez, Key-Kobad-Shakh and elsewhere. So far as we can judge, these towns continued to exist and develop without any detectable break even after the political changes already referred to; and they still survived even in the post-Kushan period.

The Ayrtam Frieze

Apart from certain material in museums (mainly coins), the first important monument of the Kushan period in the archaeology of Central Asia was the Ayrtam frieze. The first fragment of this frieze was discovered casually by a soldier who had no connection with archaeology. In October 1932, at the village of Ayrtam, on the right bank of the Amu-Darya 8 miles above

Termez, a member of the Soviet frontier forces, I. Ryasnov, noticed a carved stone slab lying in the water. The slab was fished out of the river and sent to the well-known archaeologist M.E. Masson, who studied it and in 1933 published a special monograph on the subject.

Later, in 1936, seven other fragments of the frieze were discovered at Ayrtam during excavation of the remains of a Buddhist shrine by the Termez Archaeological Expedition led by M.E. Masson. All the fragments can now be seen in the Hermitage Museum in Leningrad. The slab, of marl limestone, is some 20 inches high and has a total length of about 23 feet. On it, carved in high relief, are half-length figures of male and female musicians and bearers of offerings, each figure being framed in acanthus leaves *(Plate 49)*. The frieze is dated both by stylistic analysis and by association with a large quantity of archaeological material of the Kushan period (1st-2nd centuries) found during the excavation of the shrine. The artistic merits of this fine piece of sculpture have been generally recognised.

In addition to its work at Ayrtam the Termez Expedition also carried out excavations at Termez itself, where much valuable material belonging to the Kushan period was discovered between 1936 and 1938. We may note in particular the discovery (by E.G. Pchelina) of a Buddhist cave monastery on the hill of Kara-Tepe, where, after a long break, excavations have been successfully continued in recent years by B.Y. Stavisky. The work at Termez stimulated further exploration in this part of Central Asia, leading to the discovery of a number of remarkable sites which now occupy a prominent place in the archaeology of Central Asia.

The Ruins of Khalchayan

This town site, represented by a group of separate mounds at the village of Khalchayan in southern Uzbekistan (near the River Surkhan-Darya to the east of Termez) — one of the most important sites discovered in recent years by archaeologists working in Central Asia — is also dated to the Kushan period (1st century B.C. to 2nd century A.D.). Excavation of one of the mounds by G.A. Pugachenkova in 1962-64 revealed a well preserved small building of palace type. "Rectangular in plan, it consists of a five-bayed hexastyle *iwân*, an oblong hall beyond it, a room with two columns, and a number of adjoining apartments with linking corridor"[13] — a total of eight rooms. In this building were found stone bases for the wooden columns which had supported the roof beams, along with fire-baked tiles, antefixes and stepped merlons from the roof.

The excavations also yielded a considerable quantity of pottery, various implements and utensils, coins, etc. Of great interest were some fragments of clay sculpture which had decorated the walls of the *iwân* and the main hall. Some of this was in bas-relief, but most of it was in high relief or almost fully in the round. Altogether it formed a gallery of sculpture on a varied range of subjects. In some of the pieces Pugachenkova sees copies of figures of the classical gods and goddesses — Athena, Apollo, satyrs, etc. The items of most interest, however, are the figures of various personages who no doubt belonged to the native population of the area.

It was unfortunately not possible to establish in its entirety the original arrangement of the figures; but, arguing from the position of the fallen fragments in the general mass of debris, Pugachenkova was able to suggest the disposition of the various pieces and the interpretation of the subjects in the main hall, where the principal discoveries were made[14]. Along the top of the walls ran a frieze of garlands carried by boys like Italian *putti*, with girls, musicians, dancers, satyrs and other figures connected with the cult of Dionysus. Below the frieze were a number of sculptured groups on different themes. In one group could be distinguished the seated figures of a king and queen surrounded by their family, while above their heads hovered three divinities, including a winged figure of Nike. Another group contained no fewer than ten figures with features of strong individuality, suggesting that they were portraits of particular persons, all taking part in some solemn ceremony. Still another group, which must have occupied a large area of wall, consisted of horsemen. Fragments of six or seven horses, shown at full gallop, were found. The horsemen were clad in closely fitting belted tunics and trousers and wore soft-soled boots. On one of the fragments can be seen a hand drawing the string of a bow. Of particular interest also are the fragments of a heavily armed horseman, wearing a coat of mail made up of large metal plates and mounted on a horse covered with armour which, if Pugachenkova's interpretation is correct, is made of leather scales.

These armed horsemen at Khalchayan recall the figures of cavalrymen in the famous Parthian works of art found at Dura-Europos. They correspond to Plutarch's well-known description of the Parthian cataphracts who fought against the Romans at Carrhae in 63 B.C. In his excavation of a tomb of this period at Uygarak in the lower Syr-Darya valley S.P. Tolstov found remains of armour similar to that represented at Khalchayan.

On the same site were found a number of small plastic works and a small terracotta medallion with a stamped image of a bearded male figure seated on a throne, wearing a *kaftan* (a long belted tunic), a pointed cap and high boots. On his right stands a smaller figure in the same garb — perhaps his heir — and on his left is a small figure of Nike. The throne on which the principal figure is sitting is supported by two lions facing the spectator. The medallion is evidently a replica of a well-known piece of stone sculpture from Mathura which is identified as a portrait of Wima Kadphises, one of the early Kushan kings. A fragment of a similar piece of stone sculpture was discovered at Surkh-Kotal.

In addition to the sculpture, some small fragments of painting were also found at Khalchayan, with remains of human figures and many decorative details (foliage, flowers, vines, etc.).

It is difficult to exaggerate the importance of the discoveries at Khalchayan, and in particular of the monumental sculpture. Khalchayan represents an early stage of development of the style which Schlumberger — on the basis of the more modest remains found at Surkh-Kotal — called the "dynastic" style, as opposed to the temple art of Buddhism. In this respect Khalchayan may be classed immediately after Nisa.

Toprak-Kala

Of the sites in Khorezm belonging to the Kushan period the most interesting is Toprak-Kala. Discovered in 1938 by S.P. Tolstov, it was excavated in 1945 and subsequent years.

Toprak-Kala is a site of regular rectangular form, 550 yards long by 380 yards wide, surrounded by walls with rectangular towers. The north-west corner is occupied by a large palace, the remains of which were the principal objective of the excavations. Built of adobe brick, the palace consists of an internal courtyard surrounded by a large number of rooms of varying layout and purpose, with three towers (one each in the north-west and north-east corners and a third on the south side). Of particular interest is the group of state apartments, which are notable for their large size: the room known as the "Hall of Kings" has an area of 3,000 square feet.

In the "Hall of Kings" the excavators found a great quantity of fragments of painted clay sculpture *(Plate 51)* lying at interval along the walls. Tolstov believes that theses are figure of "the kings of Khorezm with their wives, households and patron divinities"[15]. The decoration of the hall was completed by wall paintings, which are unfortunately in poor condition; but, judging by the parts which have been preserved, they consisted partly of ornamental designs and partly of particular subjects. Remains of relief carving, and also of sculpture modelled almost fully in the round *(Plate 50)*, representing figures of kings, warriors, animals, etc., were found in some of the other state apartments. In Tolstov's opinion many of these were intended as portraits, no doubt of kings of the Khorezm dynasty. A series of apartments were identified as belonging to the royal harem. In these the walls were decorated with painting *(Plate 45)*, on the surviving fragments of which can be traced figures of musicians, women gathering grapes, etc.

The excavators also found several dozen written documents in the Chorasmian language, on wooden tablets or on leather. Most of them were of a financial and administrative nature. Some of the documents are dated according to an era whose starting point has not yet been determined.

Another feature of interest was the palace "armoury" — a workshop for the manufacture of bows.

Tali-Barzu

This site, excavated in 1936-39 by G.V. Grigoryev, produced a rich yield of material characteristic of the culture of Sogdiana. It lies 4 miles south of Samarkand, in the middle of a densely populated suburb of the town. Only part of the ancient settlement has been preserved, in the form of isolated remains of buildings and other structures, including in particular some fragments of the ramparts. The total area of the site is about 12½ acres. In the centre of the area was a large mound 60 feet high. The stratigraphical investigation of the site revealed a number of different occupation levels (T.B.I to V). Grigoryev's original dating of the site — from the 6th-5th century B.C. to the 8th century A.D. — has since proved too early. With the help of material from other sites in Central Asia it has been shown that the main Tali-Barzu levels (T.B. II and III) are to be dated to the period between the 1st and the 4th century A.D.

The wealth of material found in the excavations — fine specimens of pottery, terracotta work, seal impressions, etc. — demonstrates the high level of culture achieved in Sogdiana during these centuries. There is a very varied range of pottery vessels of excellent workmanship; the most interesting of these are jugs with a spherical body, similar in form to Greek *oenochoae*, various types of cups and goblets, vases *(Plates 38, 73, 83)*, etc. Many of these are decorated with characteristic patterns, most frequently in the form of broad bands of red and black paint. Another characteristic feature is the application of moulded ornaments, usually representing human heads and often of very delicate workmanship, under the handles of the vessels.

The Kurgan Cemeteries

All over Central Asia a large number of cemeteries belonging to nomadic tribes have been discovered, dating from the 2nd century B.C. to the 4th century A.D. These are known as *kurgan* cemeteries, from the local word for a mound or tumulus. In general each tomb is covered by one of these mounds. They are of more or less regular conical shape, usually of earth but in some areas of stone, the latter type being distinguishable above the ground only by their dimensions. The cemeteries often contain several hundred *kurgans*.

The investigations of the last few decades have shown that although these cemeteries are found throughout Central Asia their density varies considerably from area to area. They are particularly numerous in the foothill areas — Ferghana, the Semirechye, the lower Syr-Darya. They are also found on the outer fringe of the settled farming land in the western part of the Zeravshan valley, and in certain areas in the south of the Central Asian Republics.

The excavation of these tombs is relatively simple in comparison with the large Scythian *kurgans*, and of course very much simpler than the excavation of inhabited sites. The interpretation of the results, however, is fraught with great difficulty, both in relation to the chronology of the tombs and the ethnic affiliations of their occupants.

Soviet archaeologists classify the *kurgan* tombs, according to their method of construction, as the "shaft" type, the "catacomb" type, and the "underground" type. The shaft type consists of an oblong trench, in the long side of which is a recess or niche; and in this recess the body is laid. The catacomb type consists of a large vaulted chamber with a narrow entrance, which may or may not be approached by a dromos.

In the foothill areas of western Ferghana another type of tomb is frequently found along with the *kurgans*. This is the type known as *kurum* or *mug-khana*, a round stone-built chamber with an architectnral entrance and a dome-shaped roof.

Some students attach significance to the orientation of the body — the direction in which the head is pointing — which they suggest is associated with particular religious beliefs. To the author of the present work it seems probable that the orientation of the body may indicate the direction from which the people or tribe who built the tomb originally came.

The cemeteries often yield extremely valuable archaeological material *(Plates 53-55, 57-61, 65)*. In addition to clothing, various implements and utensils, ornaments *(Plates 57, 58)* and toilet articles *(Plate 53)*, the tombs were equipped with a variety of pottery and wooden vessels *(Plates 54, 59-60)* containing food (of which usually some bones of animals are preserved), and other material.

The excavations of the cemeteries have also produced considerable quantities of bones, which have been studied by anthropologists. This has shown that, in general, two anthropological types are dominant — the Europoid ("Pamir-Ferghana") type and the mixed type, with some Mongoloid characteristics. The Mongoloid features are evidence of the processes of assimilation which accompanied the movements of nomadic tribes during these centuries — processes which are also found at work in later periods of Central Asian history.

The Tup-Khona Cemetery

Archaeologists have devoted much less attention to the study of the burial practices of the settled population, and of the urban population in particular. Arrian's account of the capital of Bactria is well known, with his description of human bones lying about in the streets. The dead, he reported, were not committed to the earth but were thrown out on to the streets or cast outside the city walls. Thus, if this account is to be believed, the settled urban population did not practise the custom of burying their dead in the ground, and consequently were not concerned to erect burial mounds over their bodies.

Some authorities doubt the reliability of this account. The small number of cemeteries belonging to the urban population does, however, to some extent confirm Arrian's story. It is probable that the old tradition was maintained after the time of Alexander, although Arrian asserts that Alexander abolished the practice.

However this may be, the only cemetery belonging to the settled population of this period which has been the subject of archaeological investigation is the necropolis of Tup-Khona near Hissar (west of Dushanbe), where excavations were carried out in 1948-49 by M.M. Dyakonov.

The burials at Tup-Khona are characterised by the absence of any structure above the grave. The great majority of the tombs are dated to the Greco-Bactrian and Kushan periods. The dead were buried in a rectangular trench, lying on their backs with their heads to the north. The tombs contained various ornaments, sometimes mirrors, and often coins, which were placed in the dead man's mouth or on his chest — a practice evidently borrowed from the Greeks ("Charon's obol"). The grave was roofed over with adobe bricks.

Occasional burials carried out by settled peoples have been discovered sporadically in other parts of Central Asia. They show a number of characteristic features: thus in some cases the walls of the grave are lined with stone slabs, forming a kind of casket. Burials in terracotta sarcophagi have also been found. It is probable, too, that the practice of burying only the bones in ossuaries, after the flesh had been removed from the body, dates from this period.

FROM THE KUSHANS TO THE
ARAB CONQUEST

IV

The Historical Data

The external causes of the decline of the Kushan kingdom, as we can deduce them from the sources, are fairly obvious. They were the expansion of Sassanian Iran, the formation in India of the national state of the Guptas, and a new wave in the movement of nomadic peoples pressing into Central Asia. These events did not all take place at the same time: the Sassanian offensive against the Kushan kingdom, or at any rate the first Sassanian thrust, came in the early forties of the 3rd century, while the formation of the Gupta state and the appearance of new nomadic peoples in the political arena are to be dated not earlier than the first half of the 4th century. For the future destiny of Central Asia the most important of these three events was the movement of the nomadic peoples.

The movement in the 4th century which brought the nomads into Central Asia is to be seen as part of the great wave of nomadic movement which is known in the history of Western Europe as the Migration of the Peoples. These peoples are known by various names — the Chionites, the Huns, the White Huns, the Hephthalites. The last two designations seem to be synonymous, referring to the same people. About the Chionites there is some difference of opinion: some authorities consider them to be the same as the White Huns, others regard these as two distinct peoples. In fact the Chionites appear in only a few episodes in the history of Central Asia. Our main information about them comes from the Roman historian Ammianus Marcellinus.

According to Ammianus the Chionites occupied an area of territory to the south-east of the Caspian about the middle fifties of the 4th century. The historian saw the Chionites' camp with his own eyes during the siege of the Roman frontier town of Amida[16] in Mesopotamia by Shapur II, Shahanshah of Iran, in the year 359, when the Chionites were fighting in alliance with the Persians. Later they appear again, but this time as enemies of the Sassanid kings Varahran V (420-438) and Yazdagird II (438-457). To them, too, is attributed the final destruction of the power of the Kushans in Central Asia and northern Afghanistan.

Hephthalites and Turks

We are very much better informed about the "White Huns" or Hephthalites. A considerable body of evidence about them is available from Byzantine, Indian, Chinese, Arabo-Persian, Armenian and other written sources. In spite of this there are very varying, and sometimes contradictory, views about a number of questions in the history of the state founded by the Hephthalites. Well-informed Chinese chronicles refer to particular areas in eastern Turkestan (Turfan) as the home of the Hephthalites. According to these accounts the Hephthalites were driven out of this area as a result of a conflict with the neighbouring Zhu-zhan tribes.

The same sources put the formation of the Hephthalite state in the fifties of the 5th century. As capitals of this state the Chinese chronicles name the towns of Lan-shi and Pa-ti-yen, which it has not so far been possible to identify. Like the Kushans (the Yueh-chi) at an earlier stage, the Hephthalites directed the main impetus of their expansion towards northern India, where they came into conflict with the Gupta kingdom. The Guptas were able, however, to hold up the advance of the Hephthalites into the heart of Hindustan. The Hephthalites successfully withstood repeated attacks by the Sassanids on their territory, and in one of these campaigns King Peroz (457-484) was killed, and his successors had to bind themselves to pay a heavy tribute to the king of the Hephthalites. In this period the fortunes of Sassanian Iran sank to a low ebb. About the middle of the 6th century, however, during the reign of Khusro I (530-570), Iran recovered its economic and military strength and resumed its aggressive activities against the Hephthalites.

At the same time (i.e., the mid 6th century) a second "steppe empire", the Turkish Kaganate, was formed on the north-eastern boundaries of

Central Asia, covering a huge area from the frontiers of China to the south Russian steppes. As a result of simultaneous military operations by Khusro I and the Khâqân (Kagan, Khan) of the Turkish Empire between 563 and 565 the Hephthalite state was destroyed and its territory divided between Iran and the Turkish Kaganate. The frontier between the two ran to the west of Balkh, probably along the River Murghab.

This peaceful demarcation of spheres of influence, however, did not last long. Even during Khusro's reign there was serious friction between Iran and the Kaganate, and in the reign of Hormizd (570-590) this developed into military conflict. The highlight of these hostilities was provided by the celebrated exploits of Hormizd's general Bahram Chubin, who inflicted a crushing defeat on the Turkish forces. Being suspected of harbouring ambitious designs of his own, he fell into disgrace; whereupon he led a rising against the king and seized the throne. The Byzantine Emperor then intervened on behalf of the heir to the Sassanid throne, Khusro II, and defeated Bahram Chubin, who fled to the Turkish headquarters and was there treacherously killed. As a result of these events Central Asia remained under the control of the Turkish Kaganate.

Economic, Social and Religious Life

At this point we may consider briefly the internal condition of Central Asia under Hephthalite and Turkish rule. Perhaps the most interesting observations about the former period are to be found in the works of the Byzantine historian Procopius, who has this to say about the Hephthalites: "Although the Hephthalites are a people of Hunnish stock, they do not mingle with the Huns who are known to us, and have no communication with them... They are not nomads, like other Hunnish tribes, but have been settled in a fertile territory from time immemorial... Of all the Huns they are the only ones who are white-skinned and not hideous of countenance. In their manner of life also they differ from the other Huns, not living in such a savage fashion as they do. They are governed by a single king and form a well-ordered body politic, maintaining justice and equity among themselves and with their neighbours."[17]

To this we can add what Menander tells us about the development of an urban culture. In this respect the Hephthalites were little different from the Kushans. It is significant that according to the Chinese sources "the ruling house of the Yeh-ta (the Chinese name for the Hephthalites) was descended from the same stock as the Great Yueh-chi" — although, the chronicle goes on to add, "others say that the Yeh-ta are a branch of the Kao-chu (Kirghiz) tribe."[18] However this may be, we have certainly no evidence suggesting that during the period of Hephthalite rule in Central Asia there were any acute conflicts between the settled urban and farming culture on the one hand and the world of the nomads on the other. The available information indicates that under the Turks also the general situation in Central Asia remained stable. The Turkish Kagans, having established their base in the Semirechye, were content to maintain a general control as overlords, intervening very little in the internal affairs of the country. In some areas authority remained in the hands of local dynasties. Some of these were of Hephthalite origin; others — certainly the majority — traced their descent from the Kushan dynasty. Their subservience to the Kaganate was expressed partly in their acceptance of the overriding authority of the ruling Kagan, and apparently also in the payment of a specified tribute to the Turks — although about this we have no direct information.

The most important fact of economic life in these centuries was that international trade continued to flourish; and the Kagans consistently showed the liveliest interest in its development. In this trade, which passed along the old-established Great Silk Road, the Sogdians achieved a commanding position. The merchants of the Sogdian cities became in effect the leading promoters of international trade in this period. The thriving commerce which developed in Sogdiana led to the appearance of a string of towns founded for the purpose, stretching from the northern boundaries of

Central Asia through the Semirechye, eastern Turkestan and Mongolia to the Great Wall of China, the importance of which in the cultural development of these areas can scarcely be overrated.

The figure of a Sogdian merchant of Samarkand, Maniakh by name, who received the honorific title of *Tarkhan* from the Turkish Kagan, can be seen as a sign of the times. Having been entrusted by the Kagan with a special diplomatic mission, Maniakh visited the capitals of the Byzantine Empire and Sassanian Iran to promote the interests of Sogdian trade.

In addition to the Sogdians themselves, merchants from other regions of Central Asia were, of course, also involved in this trade. The list of embassies which E. Chavannes extracted from the chronicles of the Chinese Imperial court includes emissaries from all the princedoms of Central Asia; and, as V.V. Bartold remarked, these embassies were to a large extent trading missions.

In this period a leading part in the social structure was played by the land-owning class, the *dihqâns*. The *dihqâns* lived mainly in fortified castles, each with his own troop of retainers, whom he led into battle as part of the military forces of the princedom. In many respects the *dihqâns* resembled the knights of mediaeval Europe; but whereas in western Europe there was a sharp conflict between the interests of the towns and the feudal castles, in Central Asia, so far as we can judge, the relations between the feudal land-owning aristocracy and the merchant class never reached the stage of a collision between the two.

At this point it may be useful to quote, in slightly abbreviated form, Bartold's observations on this subject. Speaking of the general conditions of life in Central Asia before the Arab conquest, he writes: "The principal feature of this life is to be found in the domination of the territorial aristocracy (the so-called Dihqâns)... The local rulers were only the first noblemen; and even the most powerful among them were, like their subjects, known as dihqâns... The moneyed aristocracy, i.e. the merchants enriched by the caravan trade with China and other countries, apparently occupied a special position... They possessed vast estates, lived in castles, and in their position had little to distinguish them from the dihqâns."[19]

Finally we must consider the evidence about the ideological and religious situation in the country. The principal feature to be noted in this period is the absence in Central Asia of any uniform official religion under state protection. This is a fact of particular significance when it is remembered that in the neighbouring country of Iran Zoroastrianism achieved the status of a state religion at this very period; and we find the same thing occurring in Christian Byzantium.

In central Asia the situation was profoundly different. And although the written sources indicate that Zoroastrianism (the religion of the Magi) was fairly widespread, other religions (Buddhism, communities of Christians) also flourished, at least in certain areas. A still more important feature in the ideological field was the fact that Central Asia offered asylum to the adherents of such sects — heretical in the eyes of official Zoroastrian doctrine — as Manichaeism and later the Mazdakite movement, systems of an extreme dualist tendency which (particularly the latter) appealed to the masses of the people. A situation of this kind was well calculated to promote the formation of syncretic creeds; and this in fact is what occurred.

The Arrival of the Arabs

Such was the general situation in Central Asia when there appeared on its frontiers a fresh wave of conquerors, the Arabs.

If we take the middle of the 4th century A.D. as the correct date for the fall of the Kushan kingdom, then the arrival of the Arabs in Central Asia (651, the date of their capture of Merv) falls exactly three centuries later.

The history of the conquest of Central Asia by the Arabs, for which we have many written sources, has been the subject of intensive study, and the chronological course of events can be charted with an accuracy which is unattainable in earlier periods. The sources enable us to make one significant observation — that although in Iran the Arabs took roughly fifteen years (637-651) to achieve the conquest of the powerful Sassanid kingdom, the establishment of their authority in Central Asia required almost a century of determined efforts. The reason for this was that in Central Asia the Arabs encountered bitter resistance from the local population. In consequence it is not until the middle of the 8th century that we can see the emergence of the new Moslem culture which accompanied the Arab conquest. Thus the post-Kushan period in the history of Central Asia covers some four centuries, from the middle of the 4th to the middle of the 8th century.

Post-Kushan Archaeology

The accumulated archaeological material on these centuries is so considerable that it can scarcely be reviewed in its entirety even in a special monograph. All the various aspects of the archaeology of this period — the art, the architecture, and to a still greater degree the material culture — now call for separate detailed studies. Even in pre-Soviet days the archaeological evidence available included a considerable quantity of material relating to these centuries; and during the last thirty years dozens, if not hundreds, of sites have been discovered in Central Asia containing greater or lesser quantities of material belonging to the post-Kushan period. Since it is not possible in this study to make a complete survey of the field, or even to mention all the sites now known, we shall discuss only those which most fully illustrate the culture of the period.

The Fort of Balalyk-Tepe

In the period before the Arab conquest we find large numbers of isolated castles or forts appearing all over Central Asia. Forts of this kind have been investigated in Khorezm (Teshik-Kala, Yakke-Parsan, etc.), the area round Tashkent (Ak-Tepe), Ferghana (Kala-i-Bolo), Sogdiana (Kala-i-Mug and Batyr-Tepe) and the Kashka-Darya valley (Aul-Tepe). Many remains of forts have also been investigated in the Termez area (Dzhumalak-Tepe, Zang-Tepe, etc.). Although showing local variations in layout, they all represent a similar type, the dwelling and farmstead of a feudal landowner. A characteristic feature of these forts, or at any rate of most of those so far investigated, is the construction of the dwelling on an artificial stylobate or podium.

We may consider in rather more detail the fort of Balalyk-Tepe, some 10 miles north of Termez, which is typical of this form of structure. It was discovered and excavated by L.I. Albaum. It is a small building, 100 feet square, standing on a stylobate some 20 feet high, and contains 15 rooms. The most interesting of these is a small square room in the centre, 16 feet each way, with benches of pisé running round the walls. This was the reception room — the only one in the house — as is indicated by its plan and by the very interesting paintings found on the walls.

The paintings of Balalyk-Tepe are in varying states of preservation, but in general they are sufficiently well preserved to allow us to recover the whole of the subject-matter — particularly since all the paintings are devoted to the same theme, a ceremonial banquet in which a large number of people are taking part. The paintings which have been preserved on three walls contain 47 figures of men and women wearing splendid garments patterned in many colours. The figures are of two quite distinct types: in the foreground are the banqueters, represented in a variety of attitudes, either sitting with crossed legs or in a semi-reclining position; while behind them, on a smaller scale, are serving girls with large fans (?). The figures

68–70

75, 76

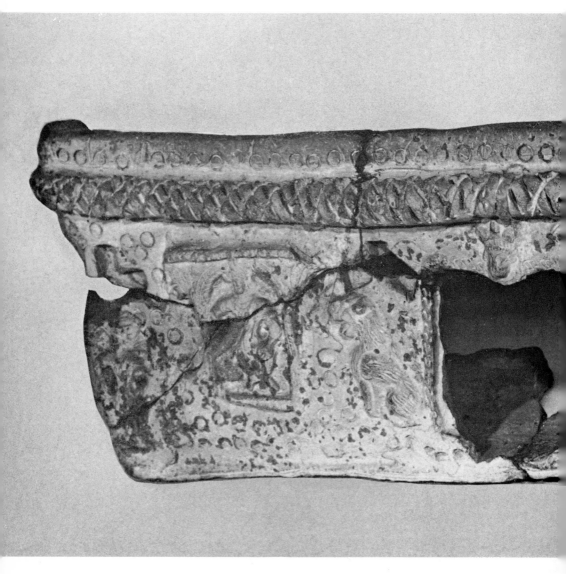

77, 78

82, 83

84, 85

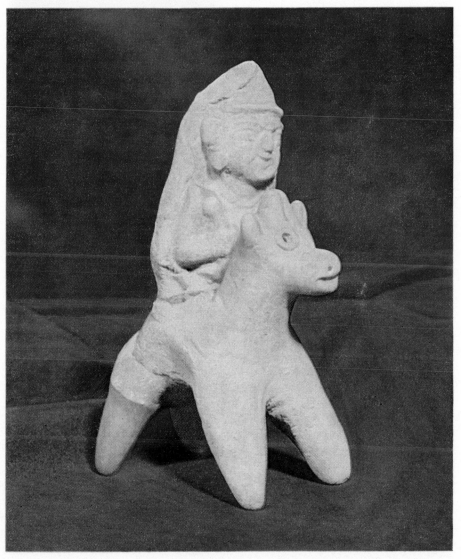

86, 87

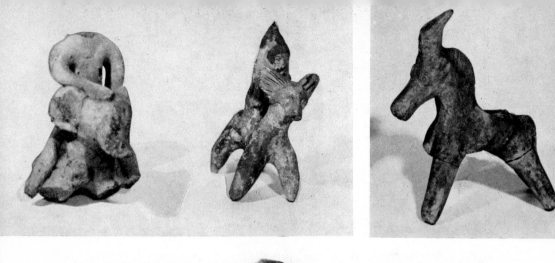

88–90

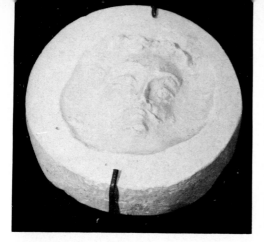
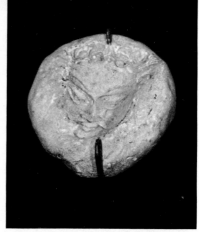

94, 95

are arranged for the most part in groups of two or three, with servants standing between the groups. The banqueters are shown either in full or three-quarter face. In one hand they hold a cup or goblet, and many of them have in the other hand a spherical object on a slender stem. At their waist the men have either a dagger in a handsome scabbard or various cases or containers, presumably for toilet articles (mirrors?). The clothing and these various articles are painted with astonishing care and delicacy. The men wear closely fitting *kaftans* with a broad lapel on the right breast; the women wear sleeveless cloaks thrown loosely over their shoulders. These garments are made of brightly-patterned fabrics, which show great variety of design, giving a striking impression of the splendid patterns in which the rich textiles of the period were woven.

The significance of this scene has been variously interpreted. Some see it as a religious rite; others think it represents a romantic episode from the well-known account in Firdausi's *Shah-nama* of the wooing of the daughters of King Sarv of the Yemen by the sons of the mythical King Faridun. Neither theory, however, can be supported by adequate evidence. As the paintings of Pendzhikent show, banqueting and battle scenes were very popular themes in the art of the aristocratic world of the period, appealing particularly to the tastes of the "knightly" feudal society.

The Shrines of Ak-Beshim and Kuva

One of the major events in Central Asian archaeology in recent years has been the discovery of Buddhist and Christian shrines in some of the peripheral regions, all of them dated to the 7th or 8th century A.D. Among the most important of these are the group of shrines discovered on the site of Ak-Beshim in the Semirechye (11 miles west of Frunze, capital of the Kirghiz Republic), consisting of two Buddhist temples and a Christian church.

Of particular interest is the Buddhist temple excavated in 1953-54 by L. R. Kyzlasov. This was a building outside the town walls (100 yards from the citadel), covering an area 250 feet by 72 feet. The excellent state of preservation of the walls, which stand up to 10 feet high, made it possible to establish the architecture of the building in almost complete detail. A considerable part of the area is occupied by a large courtyard (105 feet by 60 feet) surrounded by massive walls. Along the longer sides of the courtyard was a continuous line of cloisters in *iwân* form, apparently supported on wooden pillars. The whole building was exactly oriented to east and west. The main entrance was in the east side of the surrounding wall, in the form of a deep gatehouse with a roof borne on massive pylons. Here also were six rooms, representing dwelling accommodation and domestic offices.

The temple proper was on the west side of the courtyard. It stood on a stylobate and consisted of a rectangular octastyle hall, 60 feet long by 33 feet wide, with its principal axis running north and south. In the east wall was a wide entrance passage, and there were three other openings in the west wall — one in the centre and one at each end, leading into the principal shrine (21 feet by 11 feet) and the ambulatory which ran round it. All the temple buildings were decorated with painting and richly adorned with statues standing on pedestals and with stucco reliefs on the walls. There were also statues of gilded bronze. Unfortunately all this was found in shattered fragments; but enough was left to show that the subjects included various figures from the Buddhist pantheon, including the Buddha himself.

One find of unique importance was a whole series of openwork plaques of gilded bronze, representing various Buddhist figures framed in luxuriant patterns of vegetable ornament *(Plates 66, 67)*.

The second Buddhist temple at Ak-Beshim was excavated by L.P. Zyablin. This was smaller in size and square in plan (125 by 125 feet). A curious feature of the plan is the cruciform shape of the shrine and the two ambulatories running round it. Here were found fragments of pottery sculpture in a rather better state of preservation than in the first temple, including a very large head of the Buddha, and also traces of painting on the walls.

Inside the town of Ak-Beshim was discovered a Christian church belonging to a Nestorian community. It was a small building, 17 feet long by 16 feet wide, built on a cruciform plan in conformity with the early Syrian architectural canons. On the walls there remained, unfortunately, only traces of polychrome frescoes, the subject of which could no longer be distinguished. Christian burials were found in the courtyard and under the floor of the church itself.

Since the late 1950s excavations have been in progress on a large mediaeval town site near the village of Kuva in eastern Ferghana. A Buddhist temple, again lying outside the town walls, was excavayed here by V.A. Levina-Bulatova in 1957-58. The walls of the temple, which had been destroyed by fire, were in a much poorer state of preservation than those of the temples at Ak-Beshim. On the other hand, thanks to the fire, the numerous fragments of clay sculpture found here were in considerably better condition than at Ak-Beshim. The most interesting items were a large figure of the Buddha (or a Bodhisattva) and a large number of heads and fragments of torsos of gods and goddesses, demons and other figures typical of Mahayana Buddhist art. Some of the figures still retained traces of the original paint.

The temple was decorated with wall paintings, of which only a few small fragments had survived. Unfortunately only a preliminary account of this interesting site has been published.

The Buddhist Monastery of Adzhina-Tepe [20]

This building, the most important Buddhist monument so far discovered in Central Asia, lies in the Vakhsh valley, 11 miles east of the town of Kurgan-Tyube, in the Tadzhik Republic. Excavations have been in progress since 1960. In six years' work roughly two-thirds of the total area (100 yards by

50 yards) of this ancient mound have been cleared, which makes it possible to speak with reasonable confidence about the layout of the monastery as a whole.

The monastery consisted of two equal halves, each some 150 feet square, contiguous to one another and joined by a passage. Each half is built on a four-*iwân* plan. Within the south-eastern half is a courtyard; in the north-western half is a *stupa*. The monastery proper was in the south-eastern part. In this are the temple buildings, cells for the monks, a large hall or auditorium with an area of over 1,000 square feet, and various offices. The different parts of the structure are linked by corridors running round the inside of the perimeter.

The centre of the north-western part is occupied by a terraced *stupa* with a ramp leading up to the plinth. The *stupa* is surrounded by an outer structure consisting of long (about 50 feet) corridors running into one another at an angle, small shrines, and a number of small chapels, each with an *iwân* opening towards the *stupa*. In the corridors on the north-west side are doorways leading into six small outer shrines. The entrance to this half of the complex (which may have been the main entrance to the monastery) was in the middle of the south-east side: it consisted of a double *iwân* facing in opposite directions, linked by an arched opening.

The whole structure is built in large blocks of *pakhsa* and adobe brick (20 inches by 10 inches by 4-5 inches). The long buildings and the corridors have vaulted roofs. The square buildings (the cells and small shrines) had domed roofs, and the auditorium and temple apparently flat wooden roofs. The whole building was undoubtedly planned as a whole, and the structural design of the two halves differs only in detail.

During its period of occupation the building — and in particular the monastery part — underwent some rebuilding and reconstruction, which did not, however, make any major changes in its original plan. The rebuilding was usually required because of the collapse of the roof, and was very carelessly done: as a rule the damaged parts were made good, in part or in whole, with brick. No traces of deliberate destruction have been found.

During the excavations considerable numbers of coins (about 300 in all) were recovered. Most of these belonged to the so-called "Tocharistanian" type with a hole in the middle. Some Arab coins were also found, the latest of these being dated to the year 769.

The most interesting finds at Adzhina-Tepe were the remains of painting and sculpture. Originally there seem to have been paintings on the walls and ceilings of the buildings round the *stupa* and many of the buildings in the monastery half of the complex. Only negligible fragments were preserved *in situ* on the walls, and most of the fragments of painted stucco work were found in the piles of rubble on the floors of the various buildings. The clay sculpture of Adzhina-Tepe was better preserved *(Plates 96-98)*. This was found in the monastery temple and the small shrines round the *stupa*, as well as in niches in the corridors.

All the paintings and sculpture were on religious themes. The central feature in the sculpture and painting of Adzhina-Tepe is the image of Gautama Buddha *(Plate 96)*, but there are also representations of Bodhisattvas, monks, demonic beings and Devas. The figures are of varying size, ranging from 10-12 inches to 40 feet. The largest piece, 40 feet long, represents the Buddha reclining in Nirvana. The sculpture of Adzhina-Tepe is modelled almost fully in the round, but is designed to fit closely to the wall. The figures are enclosed in ornamental frames, and the figure of Buddha is always surrounded by a nimbus and *mandorla* in relief.

All the sculpture is moulded from clay without any reinforcement. Remains of the original colouring can still be seen. The principal characteristic of the art of Adzhina-Tepe is the combination of features of local (Central Asian) origin with traditions, themes and techniques from other areas in which Buddhism had established itself.

Remains of a Buddhist temple were discovered also at the site of Krasnaya Rechka, near the town of Frunze in the Kirghiz Republic, where a large clay sculpture of Buddha in Nirvana was found. A number of Buddhist works were also discovered in a Buddhist shrine in the Merv area.

Finally we must consider two sites which illustrate the conditions of urban life and culture in the pre-Arab period. These are Varakhsha and the ancient town site of Pendzhikent.

The Palace of Varakhsha

The discoveries on this site in 1937 created a considerable sensation in the learned world. The credit for finding it belongs to V.A. Shishkin.

The site lies 19 miles north-west of Bukhara, in the western Kyzyl-Kum, now a desert of drifting sand. Archaeological investigation has shown that in ancient times the whole of this area, covering some 200 square miles, was densely populated, and that it fell into its present state of desolation in the Middle Ages (11th-12th centuries). The surface of the desert is dotted with numerous *tepes*, which conceal the remains of towns and villages or of large isolated buildings, forts or castles. Traces of an elaborate irrigation system can still be detected.

Varakhsha — the largest single site in this area — rises above the surrounding plain to a height of 60 feet in some places, for example at the citadel. The site covers an area of some 22 acres.

Varakhsha's existence as a town can be dated roughly between the 5th and the 10th century, but some individual finds (e.g., of coins) provide evidence of occupation in both earlier and later periods. The excavations revealed the remains of structures belonging mainly to the period before the Arab conquest (7th and 8th centuries). The most important results were produced by the excavation of the palace of the Bukhar-Khudats (rulers of Bukhara), an extensive complex of buildings comprising many separate apartments serving a variety of purposes. The exploration of the palace complex yielded a considerable body of information about the architectural features of the building. In particular it enabled V.A. Nilsen, an architect who took part in the excavations, to produce a striking reconstruction of one of its principal architectural elements, the three-bayed tetrastyle portico-*iwân*.

The excavation of the main state apartments also produced discoveries of particular importance, including wall paintings which have attracted much attention from scholars *(Plates 139-141)*. The paintings were found in three rooms, known respectively as the Red Room, the East Room and the West Room. (The last of these, however, has not yet been excavated). The Red Room is a large apartment 39 feet long by 26 feet wide, with pisé benches running round the walls. The paintings begin immediately above the benches, and originally extended right up to the roof, though they are preserved only up to a height of 6 or 7 feet. The figures are painted against a red background. In the parts which have survived the paintings are divided into two bands or registers. The whole length of the lower register, which is 4 feet high, is occupied by a series of hunting scenes, spaced out at roughly equal distances from one another. The hunters are mounted on elephants of different colours, two men to each elephant — the "driver" and the central figure or hero. The two characters seem to be the same in all the scenes, but in some cases this cannot be established with certainty because of the damaged condition of the painting.

The principal character's dress seems quite unsuitable for hunting: he wears a cloak flung loosely over his shoulders, fluttering in the wind, and on his head is a richly ornamented headdress or crown. The elephants are being attacked on both sides by large felines (*Plates 139, 141*) and fantastic animals (winged griffins) *(Plate 140)*, and both the principal character and the "driver" are busily engaged in driving them off. As V.A. Shishkin observed, the artists had little idea of what elephants looked like and produced exceedingly inaccurate representations of these unfamiliar beasts.

I do not share Shishkin's view that these scenes are taken from mythology, representing the hero's fight against the forces of evil: it seems to me that the Varakhsha artists were principally concerned with achieving decorative effects. These pictures, with their warm colouring and their repetition of the same scene in a carefully contrived arrangement, create an impression of purely decorative art, more concerned with pattern and colour than with content.

Above the lower register is a second band of painting, of which only the bottom part is preserved. In this the legs of animals and birds can be distinguished: evidently the scene represented a procession of animals.

Judging from its size (56 feet long by 38 feet wide) and the remains of its wall paintings, the second room, the East Room, was the throne room, an apartment used for ceremonial receptions. All its walls were adorned with painting, but this suffered severe damage in subsequent reconstructions of the room. Only a few fragments on the south and west walls have survived in fair condition. On the west wall is a scene representing a group of warriors on horseback, riding from left to right, clad in plate armour and pointed helmets. Undoubtedly this wall was originally covered with a large battle scene containing a large number of figures.

The south wall of this room — the principal wall — was occupied by a large and crowded scene representing a state ceremonial reception. Unfortunately the painting is badly damaged, but even the few fragments that have survived are of exceptional interest. In the centre of the picture was a high throne,

101–103

supported on the crouching figures of large winged camels. From the throne hung a patterned fabric, no doubt a carpet. Of the figure seated on the imperial throne there survive only the legs, in loose trousers, and part of a garment richly decorated with pearls and gold plaques. In front of the throne, slightly to the left, can be distinguished five kneeling figures of men and women. Two of these figures — a man and a woman — are wearing garments of brightly patterned cloth. The man wears a sword and a dagger in rich scabbards, and the heads of both figures are surrounded by nimbuses. In front of them is a tall bronze sacrificial altar or incense brazier, of complicated design, from the bowl of which rise tongues of flame. The man seems to be pouring aromatic oil into the bowl from a spoon, and the woman holds a decorated chalice in her hands.

The ornament on the outside of the brazier is of remarkable quality. In the centre, under an arch, is the figure of a woman seated on a throne which is constructed in the shape of a crouching camel. The rest of the surface is decorated with a variety of vegetable and geometric ornament. On the other side of the brazier is the kneeling figure of a man, richly dressed and with a dagger at his waist.

The excavation of the palace at Varakhsha also yielded striking specimens of another type of artistic production — decorative stucco work. Unlike the wall painting, the stucco was not found *in situ*, but in the form of a great mass of fragments, often of minute size. Originally the stucco panels had covered the upper parts of the walls, but we can only guess at the general effect of the decoration: on the evidence we have we can do no more than identify a few particular themes. The feature which immediately strikes us is the large quantity of geometric and vegetable ornament; but there were also a considerable number of other subjects, including processions of animals and birds and hunting scenes.

The distinctive qualities of the Varakhsha stucco work were well stated by V.A. Shishkin, whose assessment I should like to quote. "The special characteristic of the alabaster decoration of Varakhsha," he writes, "is the absence of meticulous finish, the rather sketchy manner, which puts it into a completely different category from later examples of this type of architectural decoration, in which the painstaking, scrupulous finish of each trifling detail is carried to a pitch of extreme virtuosity. This is true even of such important elements of the design as human faces. The mouth is sketched in with a few strokes of the knife. The eyes are often represented only by almond-shaped convexities without any further detailing. The hair, the beard, the clothing and ornaments are depicted with the same economy and understatement, in a few bold strokes. And yet we are constantly struck by the mastery and inventiveness of the artists in their treatment of their material and by the extraordinary expressiveness of the modelling".[21]

The discovery of these works of monumental art in the palaces of the Bukhar-Khudats was the most important result of the excavation of pre-Arab Varakhsha; but excavations elsewhere on the site — particularly in the citadel, which had shared the fate of the palace — also yielded other finds of great scientific value.

The exterior of the citadel shows an interesting architectural feature. The building stands on a high trapezoidal stylobate, and its external walls are in a "goffered" pattern: that is, a pattern of half-columns placed close to one another in pairs, the tops of each pair being linked by a small arch. This technique was widely used in some parts of Central Asia, for example in Khorezm and southern Turkmenia. In later periods it was used in buildings constructed of baked bricks. There is some difference of opinion about the functional and structural significance of this technique, but one thing is certain: buildings constructed on this principle were of striking architectural effect and achieved lightness without any loss of solidity.

Pendzhikent

The ancient urban site of Pendzhikent occupies a special position in the archaeology of Central Asia. The settlement was abandoned by its inhabitants as a result of the Arab conquest between the twenties and the seventies of the 8th century. It has yielded evidence on many aspects of urban life and culture in pre-Moslem Asia; and it is, therefore, worth while considering the Pendzhikent material in rather more detail.

The ancient city of Pendzhikent, the ruins of which lie on the outskirts of the present-day town of the same name, 40 miles east of Samarkand, came to the notice of archaeologists following the discovery of the famous collection of Sogdian archives on Mount Mug. These archives, as was established when some of the documents were deciphered, belonged to the last ruler of the small princedom of Pendzhikent, Divastich.

Systematic excavation of the site (*Plates 124-125*) was undertaken after the war, in 1946, by a joint expedition organised by the Institute of Archaeology of the Soviet Academy of Science, the Institute of History of the Tadzhik Academy of Science and the Hermitage Museum, under the leadership of Professor A.Y. Yakubovsky.

The ruins of ancient Pendzhikent form a complex archaeological pattern, consisting of four clearly demarcated areas — the ruler's citadel, the town proper or *shahristan*, a suburban settlement and the necropolis.

On the evidence of the excavations Pendzhikent came into existence as an urban settlement, surrounded by a defensive wall, in the 5th or early 6th century A.D. and, as already noted, was abandoned at the time of the Arab conquest of Central Asia. Thereafter no attempt was made to re-establish the town, and in consequence the uppermost building level remained intact. This circumstance determined the technique of excavation adopted on this site.

The main object of the excavations has been to carry out the fullest possible examination of the site on the last building level. This is the first time in the history of Central Asian archaeology that excavators have been faced with a situation of this kind, and the successful completion of the work is undoubtedly of major significance for the solution of a whole complex of problems connected with the history of urban life and culture in Central Asia in the pre-Moslem period.

Architecture

After many years of excavation at Pendzhikent the archaeologists have accumulated a mass of material of all kinds, which throws light not only on the material culture of the city but also on some significant features of its social and economic structure. The special value of this material lies in its comprehensiveness.

The exceptional opportunities offered by Pendzhikent as an archaeological site have made it possible in particular to study the architecture of the town with a degree of completeness which is rarely attainable. This study has been carried out by V.L. Voronina, an architect associated with the expedition, who has published a number of special studies on the subject.

The chief building materials used at Pendzhikent were rectangular adobe bricks, of regular but not strictly uniform shape (on average 20 inches by 10 inches by 4 ½ inches) and blocks of beaten clay *(pakhsa)* roughly 40 inches square. The walls of the buildings were built of clay blocks, the vaulted roofs of brick. Occasionally domed roofs, also of brick, are found. The builders of Pendzhikent also developed a type of raftered roof, usually supported on wooden columns, which in Voronina's reconstruction is of the shape known as a "lantern" roof. Stone was, for all practical purposes, not used in building: occasionally, but rarely, stone column bases were found. Baked brick in the form of tiles was used for facing walls and covering floors*, but this is also rare.

The dwelling houses were of two stories. The houses belonging to different social classes are fairly clearly distinguished both by the dimensions and

---

* In some cases there is evidence for the use of baked tiles for roofing.

layout of the rooms and by the decoration of the interior. A characteristic feature of the houses of the wealthier classes is the tetrastyle reception room, usually of considerable size (up to 850 square feet or more), with benches of beaten clay running round the walls. In these rooms the walls were usually covered with painting from top to bottom, and the columns, joists and roof beams, door frames and doors were richly decorated with splendid carving.

Adjacent to these rooms were vaulted lobbies or passages, the walls of which were sometimes also covered with painting; and these passages communicated in turn with various ancillary rooms and domestic offices, usually also vaulted. A characteristic feature of the architecture of Pendzhikent is the special type of staircase with a spiral ramp borne on sloping arches which leads up to the rooms on the upper floor.

The rooms on the upper floor are, of course, much more poorly preserved than those on the ground floor. From the remains found in all the excavated areas, however, it can be determined that these upper rooms were mainly living quarters, conveniently arranged for everyday domestic purposes. Frequently the houses contained special rooms, either on the lower or the upper floor, which apparently served as private chapels and had a special altar niche built into one wall, with space for a hearth.

The excavators found two examples of rooms containing a large platform or dais designed, in the author's view, for theatrical performances or dancing. The most elaborate dwelling houses had façades in the form of *iwâns* borne on columns or of loggias with semi-domed roofs.

In addition to houses of this type, which evidently belonged to the most prosperous citizens, the districts in the eastern part of the *shahristan* and, to an even greater extent, the excavated areas in the southern part of the town contain houses of a much more modest character, both in layout, the number and size of the rooms, and the internal decoration. These houses have none of the fine reception rooms with their rich decoration and have no *iwâns;* but they too were of two stories.

A distinctive feature of the suburban settlement is that each house stands by itself, so that each could be built to an individual plan to meet the owner's particular requirements. All the houses so far excavated differ from one another in layout, though in constructional style and technique they are similar to the general run of houses in the town. These houses too are built on two floors.

The Pendzhikent excavations revealed for the first time the local type of temple architecture, which differs fundamentally from the cult buildings of the Buddhists or Christians, and also from the fire temples which are familiar in Iran. The temples consisted of an elaborate complex of separate buildings linked by large courtyards, the main temple buildings being erected on stylobates within the courtyards. They were tetrastyle structures open to the east, joined by a passage to the *cella* on the west side and surrounded on three sides by corridors or open galleries. All along the east front was a hexastyle *iwân*, forming in effect an extension of the principal chamber. The courtyards were enclosed partly by a wall and partly by buildings serving a variety of purposes.

The excavations also yielded information about the premises occupied by shopkeepers and craftsmen. In general these were small detached single-storey buildings.

The architecture of Pendzhikent as a whole is remarkable for the great variety of types of building serving different functions, the advanced constructional techniques, and the marked concern with the amenities of urban life. The buildings demonstrate the relatively high level of material prosperity achieved by the population of the town, and this is also shown by the great quantity of material found in the excavations *(Plates 72, 77, 80, 84, 85, 110, 113, 117-119, 122-123)*.

Material Life

At Pendzhikent, as at other settlements excavated in Central Asia, the material found in greatest quantity was pottery *(Plates 80, 84, 85, 123)*. Extraordinary numbers of vessels of different types were discovered, serving a great variety of purposes. They included kitchen and table ware in a wide range of shapes and sizes, large jars *(khums)* for the storage of liquids or dry substances, water jugs, miniature jars in a variety of shapes designed to contain spices, toys, etc. Many of these vessels, particularly the table ware, are remarkable for their elegance of form and variety of decoration. Many of them imitate similar vessels in metal. Vases of this kind were in particular favour with the citizens of Pendzhikent.

Quite large numbers of glass objects were also found. As a rule, however, these were small articles, mainly bottles.

Iron objects were also found in considerable quantity and great variety. They included various tools and implements, weapons, pieces of harness, and a wide range of domestic implements and utensils.

Many bronze objects were found. Apart from a number of larger objects (a candlestick, a massive pestle), they were mainly toilet articles and ornaments (rings, ear-rings, bracelets, a variety of pendants, mirrors, belt ornaments, etc.). Relatively few articles made from the precious metals (ornaments such as rings and ear-rings) were found. There was also a great variety of beads and gems made of semi-precious stones (cornelian, turquoise, lapis lazuli, agate, various red stones, etc.). Many bone articles of various kinds were also found.

This list of the types of objects found is, of course, by no means completely representative. The circumstances in which Pendzhikent perished — the wars, the repeated risings, the burning and pillaging, the departure of the inhabitants — led to the destruction of immense quantities of material. In addition there was another factor which contributed to the disappearance of whole categories of objects which would have thrown light on the material culture of the town — the loess soil of Pendzhikent, in which articles made of organic materials are totally destroyed. This applies particularly to cloth and to leather and wooden articles.

A rich store of information about the culture of Pendzhikent—mainly, it is true, the culture of the ruling classes—is provided by the works of art discovered in the town, particularly the painting. The paintings are especially valuable for the information they give about clothing and the patterns of textiles and carpets, of which it would be difficult or impossible to obtain even an approximate idea from excavated material. They add significantly to our knowledge of the types of jewellery and ornaments worn by the people of Pendzhikent.

The paintings also give us a considerable body of most valuable information about weapons, both defensive and offensive, and horses' harness. There are many representations of various types and shapes of metal vessels (evidently of silver and gold), of architectural structures, and of various types of furniture, including kings' thrones. The paintings also depict articles of temple furniture of which nothing was previously known. Some of these objects are of outstanding artistic quality.

The evidence of the paintings is of particular value because—as we can see by comparing some of the objects excavated with the representation of the same objects in paintings—the artists reproduced their models with great accuracy, down to the most minute details. This is a feature characteristic of the whole art style of this period.

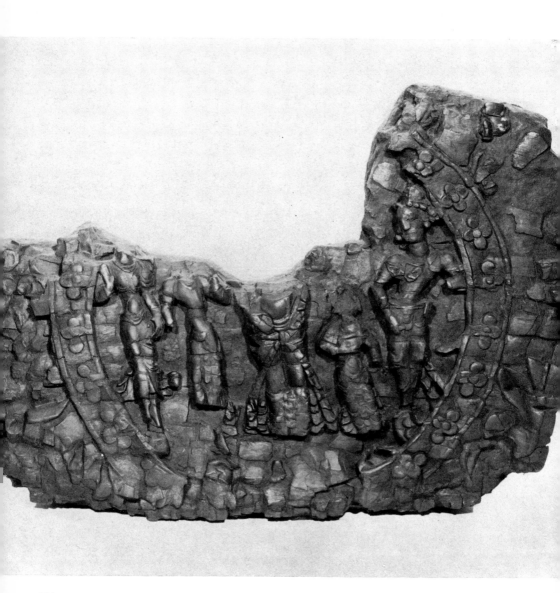

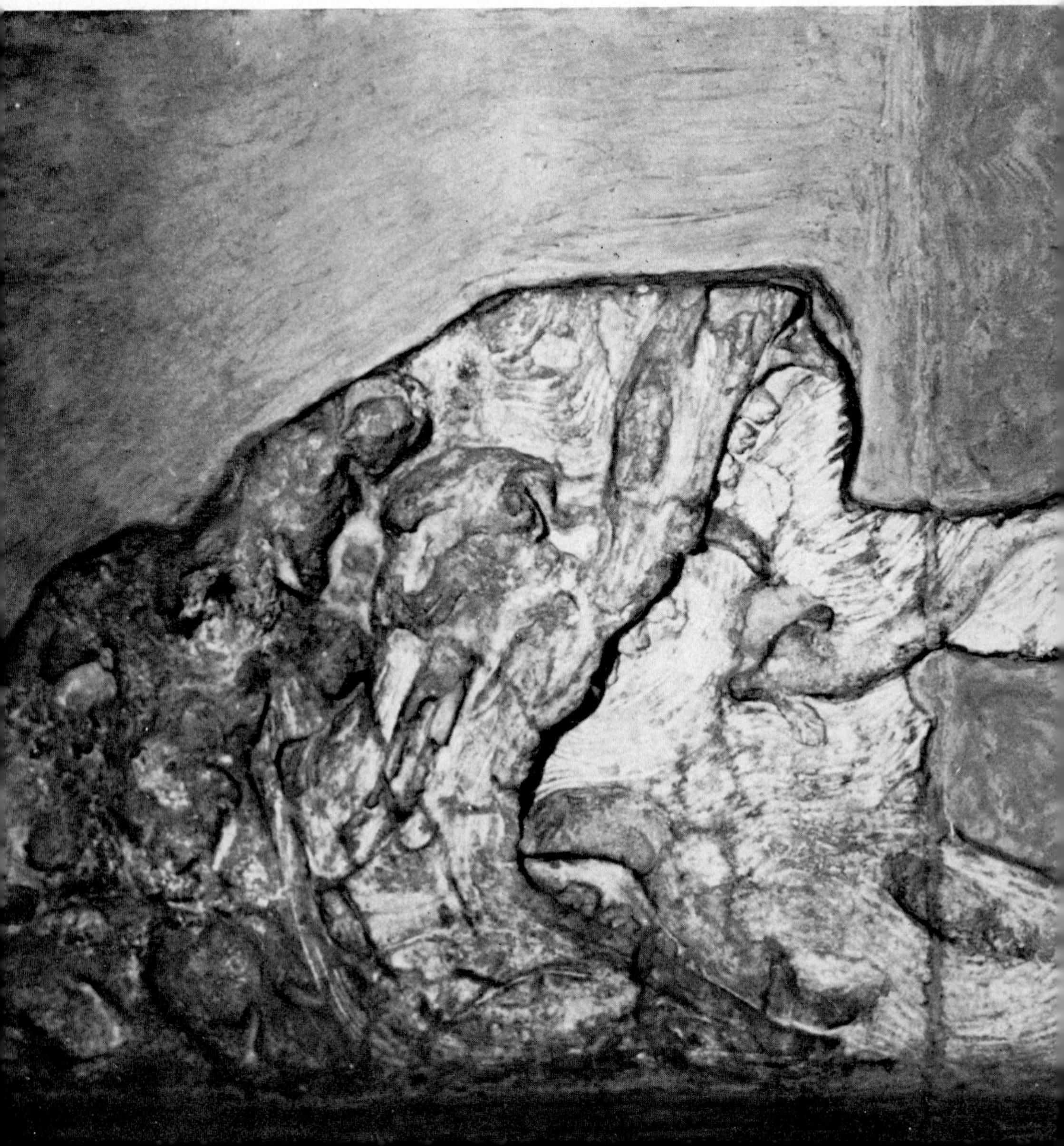

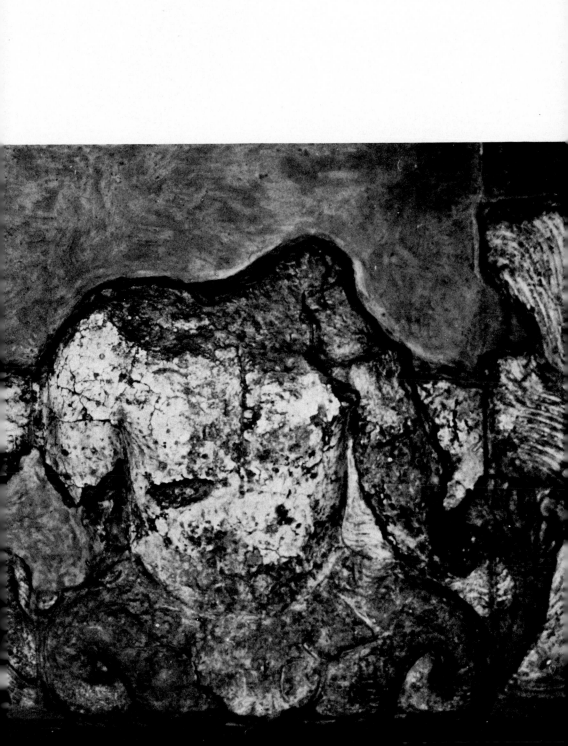

119   117

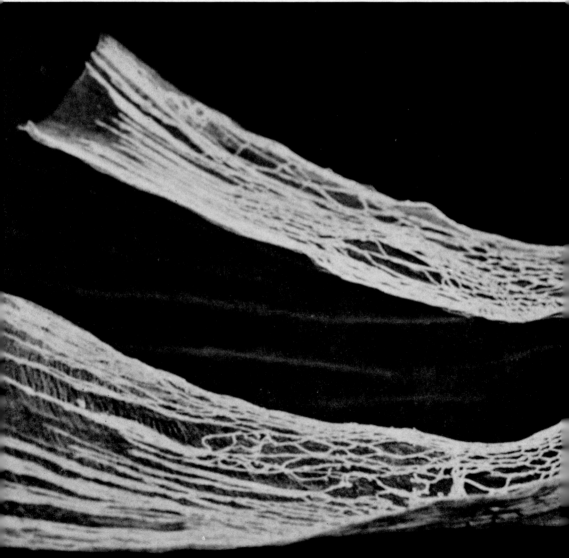

118

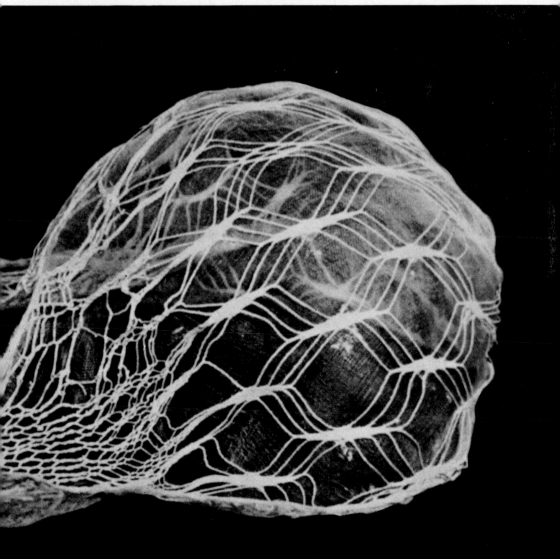

122, 123

129, 130

Written Records

Particularly good evidence of the general level of culture achieved by the people of Pendzhikent is provided by two kinds of material—literary documents and works of figurative art.

The wide diffusion of the art of writing, and consequently of literacy in the Sogdian language spoken by the population of the town, is demonstrated by the archive documents from the castle on Mount Mug and the widely distributed inscriptions on pottery sherds and stones. The inscriptions on pottery were sometimes incised before firing, but in most cases were written in black paint on the finished article. The inscriptions on stone were either incised or painted. Finally there were inscriptions on the walls of buildings.

It is of interest to consider the content of these inscriptions.

The documents which have been the subject of the most detailed study are the archive documents from Mount Mug. What mainly emerges from these is the elaborate development of official documentation and correspondence, including diplomatic letters, reports, legal documents (e.g., marriage contracts and leases) and administrative and financial records. There are also a number of astronomical and astrological texts (calendars) of great interest.

It is evident, of course, that these surviving remains are by no means representative of the general body of literature. We need only consider, for example, the finds of Sogdian texts in eastern Turkestan, which are quite clearly evidence of a general Sogdian culture. These texts indicate that there were translations into the Sogdian language of the teachings of various religious faiths, Buddhist, Manichaean and Christian. Unfortunately the texts of medical, mineralogical and astronomical works have been preserved only in small fragments.

Certain documents found in eastern Turkestan—extracts from the famous Indian collection, the *Panchatantra*, and records of local epic legends in the Sogdian language—are of great interest to students of cultural history. We can take it as certain that these texts were known in Pendzhikent, since the paintings discovered by the excavators drew their themes from works of this kind.

Art

Pendzhikent also occupies a prominent place among the archaeological sites in Central Asia on which works of monumental art have been discovered. The works found here are of three types—large-scale wall paintings in many colours, wood-carving, and clay sculpture. In quantity of material the wall paintings come first *(Plates 132-138, 142-145)*. Paintings, or traces of paintings, have been found in more than fifty rooms. These paintings, in a rich spectrum of colour, were used to decorate the walls of both temples and dwelling houses. The paintings covered the whole surface of the walls from top to bottom, frequently being divided into a number of separate bands or registers. Many of the rooms decorated with painting were reception rooms with a wall area of 500 square feet or more.

It is evident that the paintings which have survived represent only a fraction of the great store of art treasures which must have existed originally. Many painted rooms were destroyed by fire, and in these the paintings have usually been lost. In such cases the only evidence we have of their existence consists of small patches of colour and the outlines of a few individual figures which can still be traced. But even in rooms which have not suffered from fire the paintings have survived only in fragments, varying in size and state of preservation. Nevertheless the quantity of material that has come down to us in reasonably good condition is still very considerable.

The second category of monumental art is wood-carving *(Plates 106-109, 111, 112, 114, 115)*. In contrast to the wall paintings, we owe our knowledge of these works to the fires which destroyed the buildings containing them. Much of the wood in these buildings, including pieces of carving, was merely charred and not completely consumed, and was then buried under a thick layer of debris which helped to preserve it. In areas untouched by fire, wood and other organic materials decomposed completely in the loess soil, leaving only a layer of dust.

Remains of wood-carving, rather poorly preserved, were found in seven rooms. Like the wall paintings, they are of high artistic quality and cover a varied subject-matter. Two types of treatment are found—relief carving, in various degrees of high and low relief, and sculpture carved almost completely in the round.

So far as we can judge from the material at present available, clay sculpture *(Plates 99-105, 116)* did not enjoy great favour in Pendzhikent: at any rate no trace of it has been found elsewhere than in the temple buildings. In the temples, however, clay sculpture seems to have occupied a place of honour. This is shown by the existence of special niches, both in the principal and subsidiary chambers of the temples, which were undoubtedly intended for pieces of sculpture. Unfortunately in only one of these niches was there found a small fragment of the sculptured figure which had originally stood there. Some idea of the nature of this clay sculpture can be gained from the material found in the outer *iwân* on the wall of the second temple. One important find was a carved panel in high relief, some 30 feet long and 3 feet high.

Subjects and Themes

As already noted, one of the main characteristics of the works of art found at Pendzhikent is the extraordinarily wide range of subjects. In almost every one of these works we encounter a new theme, or a new treatment of a theme already known. Within the framework of this study it is clearly not possible to give even the most summary account of all the material discovered. We shall, however, attempt to sketch out a general classification of the material, noting the most characteristic types of theme—which are, of course, significant evidence on the culture of the period.

One type of theme frequently used by the Pendzhikent artists was taken from the epics. The epic legends provided them with a ready supply of material, enabling them to depict whole cycles of episodes connected with one general theme or one particular hero. A typical example of this is offered by a large-scale composition, of which roughly half has been preserved, showing a series of scenes representing the exploits of one particular *bogatyr* (epic hero) and his followers. From the nature of the episodes and the representation of the principal figure we can assert with fair confidence that in this painting the artist is depicting a series of adventures of Rustam, the famous hero of the Sacian (Central Asian) epic, whose glory was to be celebrated rather more than two centuries later in Firdausi's great poem, the *Shah-nama* ("Book of Kings") *(Plates 136-138)*.

Themes from the ancient epics are also found in a series of episodes representing either full-scale battles or single-handed combats between young female warriors and men—clearly a reminiscence of the legends about the Amazons.

The painting, wood-carving and clay sculpture of Pendzhikent also reflect various religious creeds and cults and their associated rituals, with representations of various heavenly bodies—the sun, the moon and the planets—and the symbolic figures in which they were incarnated. They also reveal some of the basic features of the ideology of the population of Pendzhikent—a problem to which very little attention has so far been given.

The art of Pendzhikent also provides evidence of the penetration of foreign cults. Thus some paintings depict cult figures represented in a form which indicates their Hindu (Saivite) origin.

The artists of Pendzhikent drew their material also from folklore and the fabulous animal epics, still alive in our own day in the form of fairy tales—for example scenes showing the hero freeing a girl from a tree in which she has been imprisoned by her wicked step-mother's spells, or a picture showing the bird of good fortune carrying golden eggs—a theme which has become part of the folklore of the world.

Of particular interest is a small picture showing a hare who by his persuasive eloquence has induced a lion to jump into a deep lake, and has thus freed the animals from his tyranny. This attractive little scene illustrates very exactly a fable from the well-known Indian collection, the *Panchatantra*.

Many of these works also illustrated scenes from the everyday life of the period—feasts *(Plates 142-145)*, single–handed combats, hunting, board games similar to the popular Oriental game of *nard*, wrestling, and so on.

THE MAIN PROBLEMS

Problems of Acculturation and Socio-economic Problems

The particular problems of any given period are, of course, peculiar to that period. In this survey it is not possible, nor is it necessary, to review all the problems presented by Central Asian archaeology: I propose, therefore, to discuss only a few of the most significant questions.

The intensive investigations of Neolithic and Bronze Age sites (early agricultural cultures) have given rise to much discussion of the local peculiarities of the cultures of these periods in their different areas of diffusion, their relations with similar cultures outside Central Asia, and the processes which led to the integration of these local cultures. As already noted, three or four main areas belonging to these cultures are now distinguished in Central Asia—the south-western area (part of southern Turkmenia), the northern area (the deltas of the Amu-Darya and the Syr-Darya), the eastern area (Ferghana) and the south-eastern area (the mountainous parts of Tadzhikistan).

While the cultures of the south-western area in the course of their development show links with the similar cultures of the Near East (Iran, Mesopotamia, etc.), the cultures of the northern area are closely connected genetically with the Bronze Age cultures of the great belt of steppe which extends from the southern Urals to the headwaters of the Yenisey, the area occupied by the Andronovo culture (20th-10th centuries B.C.), which has been so fruitfully studied by archaeologists working in Kazakhstan and southern Siberia. In the Bronze Age culture of Ferghana links have been observed with the cultures of the areas east of the Ferghana valley. Finally, the distinctive culture of the south-eastern mountain areas—the Hissar culture—is marked by local features determined by the geographical conditions of the mountainous country in which it is found.

By analysing the level of culture in the different areas archaeologists have been able to demonstrate the lack of uniformity in their development. In particular the civilisation of the south-western area shows a significantly higher level than other parts of Central Asia.

At the same time there are quite distinct resemblances between the culture of the south-western area, at any rate during the main painted pottery stage, and the similar cultures in the neighbouring parts of northern India, on such sites as Quetta and Nad-i-Ali in Afghanistan. This led V.M. Masson to suggest the possibility of a movement of population from Central Asia to the frontiers of India, associated with the problem which has long exercised historians—the conquest of India by Aryan peoples. But, as Masson rightly points out, the correctness of this hypothesis cannot be established because there has been so little study of the archaeology of eastern Iran and the neighbouring parts of Afghanistan, a region which— particularly in relation to the prehistoric cultures—is still a blank on the archaeological map.

The investigation of sites belonging to the transitional stage between the prehistoric and historical periods and to the historical periods themselves has also raised a large number of very important problems. Specialist students are concerned, for example, to determine with the help of archaeological evidence the date of emergence of a class society, the time when social strata differentiated according to their possession of wealth, the ownership of private property, and the first embryo of a state organisation made their appearance within the primitive tribal community. Evidence of these processes is provided by the appearance of fortified citadels within the town sites, the discovery of tombs with rich grave goods which set them apart from the ordinary burials, the great quantities of seals found in the excavations, and the marked professionalisation of craft industry.

A more difficult problem to solve with the aid of archaeological data—and for the early historical periods this is the only evidence available—is that of determining the nature of the different social classes. In Soviet historical

132, 133

142

143, 144

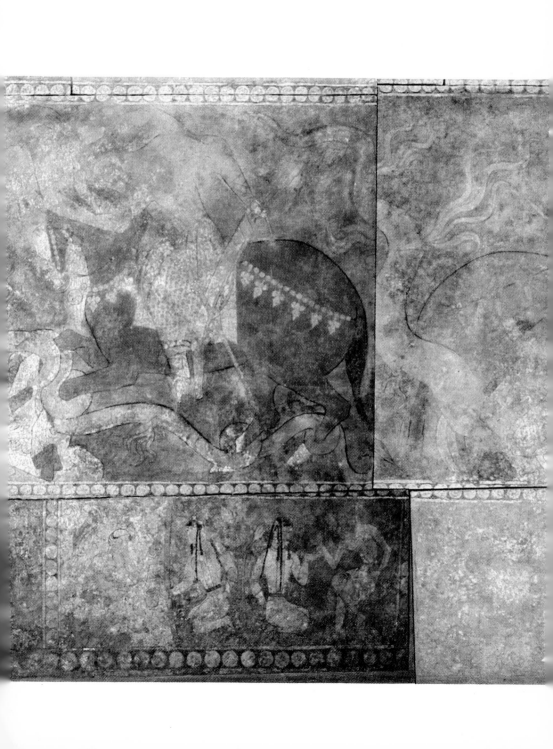

literature the predominant view is that the first society in Central Asia organised on a class basis was a slave-owning society. In support of this view can be adduced the evidence provided by the development of irrigation in Central Asia. The construction of large-scale irrigation systems, say the proponents of this theory, could be achieved only with the help of great masses of slaves. But to many scholars, including the author, this argument seems unconvincing, at any rate in relation to Central Asia. The question, therefore, is still open.

One of the most important problems of the historical periods is that of the relationships between the nomadic tribes and the settled population, on which there is an extensive literature. The contribution made by archaeology to the solving of this important historical problem can hardly be overestimated. The material recovered by archaeologists in excavations of the cemeteries of the nomadic tribes and the settlements of the sedentary population led to a review of the widely accepted view about the inevitability of conflict between these two different worlds. The principal result of the contact between the two groups was an intensive process of settlement of substantial numbers of nomads on the land, which in turn led to their ethnic and cultural assimilation. But even apart from this process the co-existence of the mutually complementary nomadic and sedentary economies was a continual and valuable stimulus to trade and exchange, always an important factor in the economic life of the area. At the same time the integration of the social and political institutions of the sedentary and the nomadic worlds went forward. All this led to the elimination of the conflicts between them, as was most conspicuously demonstrated in the critical periods of their history when they were fighting against foreign enemies.

Problems of Art History

In this section we shall be concerned with two problems, the emergence of which is a direct result of the archaeological discoveries of the last thirty years. The first of these is the problem of the genesis of Central Asian monumental art.

Until the thirties of this century the monumental art of Central Asia was practically unknown. An excellent illustration of this is provided by the well-known work, *A Survey of Persian Art*, published in 1938. In this work only one plate out of 257 was devoted to the pre-Moslem art of Central Asia[22]. Moreover this one plate illustrated mainly terracottas and a few other small pieces of plastic art; and even these were regarded, in the main, as a provincial reflection of Iranian art.

At the present time, following the discovery, in different parts of Central Asia, of so many examples of monumental sculpture and painting belonging to many different periods, this attitude is no longer tenable. It is now quite clear to anyone who approaches the matter with an open mind that Central Asia had its own independent artistic tradition, with roots going back to a very remote period. It is true that some of the links in this tradition, particularly in the earlier periods, are still missing. Thus we must still rely on Chares of Mitylene, a contemporary of Alexander the Great, for the information that the temples, palaces and private residences of the "barbarians living in Asia" frequently contained pictures on epic themes. From this statement it has been concluded that "in the Achaemenian period, alongside the art of the court—wholly under foreign influence and quite alien to the ordinary people—there existed a school of popular art, which in later times was strong enough even to withstand Greek influence."[23] The archaeological evidence is not yet sufficient to entitle us to pronounce definitely on the correctness of this assertion; but what is already known about the art of later periods does, in the author's opinion, provide indirect support for the view.

We move on to firmer ground when we consider the art of the Parthian and Kushan period.

We are indebted to Professor Rostovtzeff[24] for the recognition of the Parthian period as an independent stage in the development of the art of Iran, based mainly on an analysis of the evidence from sites in the western provinces of the Parthian kingdom (Dura-Europos, Hatra, etc.). The discovery of the art of Nisa showed that this period was of equal significance in "eastern Iran" (i.e., Central Asia).

We are now entitled to regard the Kushan period as one of outstanding importance in the history of art. The key sites of this period are Surkh-Kotal in southern Bactria (northern Afghanistan) and, to an even greater degree, Khalchayan in northern Bactria (southern Uzbekistan).

The discovery of Surkh-Kotal, now familiar to scholars throughout the world, was the work of the French archaeologist Daniel Schlumberger. To him also we owe a new solution of the important problem of the origin of the art of Gandhara and the art schools contemporary with it which flourished in Afghanistan and northern India. This problem has a direct bearing on the history of Central Asian art; for it is in the art of Gandhara that scholars have seen the roots of Central Asian art in the following period. We need not concern ourselves here with current theories about the origin of the art of Gandhara itself and the assessment of its status: we may merely note that these theories have been unable to provide satisfactory answers to many problems posed by the art of the Gandhara school itself. Schlumberger's view is that during the Kushan period there developed in certain parts of the Kushan kingdom schools of art which had certain affinities with one another in a number of respects, and particularly in relation to the styles they favoured. The differences which can be observed between one region and another are due to some local tradition or substratum which reflects an earlier stage in the development of art. While for the Indian school of Mathura this was the tradition of Indian art, for the school of northern Afghanistan the substratum was, in Schlumberger's view, the earlier school which he called Greco-Iranian.

In applying the term "Iranian" to Afghanistan (or, more correctly, Bactria) Schlumberger was following a tradition from which western European scholars are unable to break free. In fact, however, Schlumberger himself shows some awareness of its unsoundness. Thus he notes that no factual data to confirm his view are available in Iran itself—i.e., central and eastern Iran—and recommends that attention should be given to the countries bordering on Iran. "We ought not," he says, "to disregard completely the Iranian world of southern Russia, and we ought to give proper weight to the Soviet discoveries in Turkestan and in Armenia."[25]

He suggests that the art of these schools as a whole should be given the name of Kushan art. As he himself stresses, this name—in my own view a very suitable one—covers two different types of art: temple art (i.e., Buddhist art) and court art or, as Schlumberger calls it, "dynastic" art. In introducing the conception of Kushan art Schlumberger is, in my opinion, opening up great possibilities both for the study of the art of the Kushan period itself and for our understanding of the later development of art in the areas which formed part of the Kushan kingdom, including parts of Central Asia. From this point of view particular significance attaches to the discovery by the Soviet archaeologist G.A. Pugachenkova of the site at Khalchayan (mentioned above, page 99), which belongs to roughly the same period as Surkh-Kotal (probably slightly earlier) and is also geographically close to Surkh-Kotal.

The art of Khalchayan can be recognised at once as a courtly and secular art. In the light of the preceding discussion we may reasonably conclude that the art of this period was the basis of the later development which led to the formation of a number of distinctive schools of Central Asian art. Thus in the clay sculpture of Surkh-Kotal, and still more in that of Khalchayan, we recognise at once a direct ancestor of the court sculpture of Toprak-Kala in Khorezm. There is nothing surprising in this, since the Toprak-Kala sculpture is the closest in time to the Kushan period. But even in later Central Asian works of the early mediaeval period the influence of Kushan art can be detected with equal certainty.

This is true also of the Buddhist art of Ak-Beshim, Kuva and Adzhina-Tepe, and of the secular art of Balalyk-Tepe, Varakhsha and above all Pendzhikent. We may note that the maintenance of the traditions of the courtly art of the Kushans was helped by the fact that the ruling houses of the Central Asian princedoms in the early mediaeval period claimed descent from the Kushan dynasty. At the courts of these princely families of the later period, and in the art of those courts, the Kushan traditions were preserved with particular steadfastness.

Clearly, of course, this living art could not rely solely on traditions inherited from the past. A striking example of this is provided by Pendzhikent. Here we see a significant new phenomenon which is clearly an important step forward in the development of world art. The art of Pendzhikent emerged from the temples and from the prince's palace and found its audience among the general body of citizens. This is the explanation of the extraordinary variety of subject-matter which strikes us in the art of Pendzhikent. No doubt the patrons of this art were still to be found in the upper levels of society; and no doubt the art they favoured reflected the narrow interests, tastes and ideology of this particular stratum of the population of the town. Yet the fact remains that the art of Pendzhikent has passed beyond the restricted conception of courtly art, the idea of art as a form of dynastic propaganda, which is found, for example, in Sassanian Iran.

In suggesting, however, that the early mediaeval art of Central Asia is a natural development from the starting-point provided by Kushan art, I do not mean that the origin of all its specific characteristics is to be sought in Kushan art. We must not forget that Kushan art itself did not develop in a vacuum: as we have already noted, it absorbed the achievements of an earlier period. Nor did the development of Central Asian art come to a halt in the post-Kushan period: on the contrary, it continued to advance.

Central Asia was not isolated from neighbouring countries, either in the pre-Moslem period or later, and its art certainly did not develop in isolation. There was a constant interaction between its culture and the cultures of neighbouring peoples, with whom it had close political and economic relations. A number of students—for example, the Italian scholar M. Bussagli[26]—now recognise the influence of Sogdian art on the art of eastern Turkestan, basing themselves on the Pendzhikent material. Nor is it open to doubt that certain elements in the art of the early mediaeval period in Central Asia are to be attributed to the influence of such potent centres of artistic creation as India under the Guptas or Sassanian Iran. Nevertheless in the present state of knowledge it is legitimate to conclude that the main features of the art of Central Asia in the pre-Arab period sprang from a process of natural development of local traditions inherited from the art of the Kushan kingdom.

Problems in the History of Religion

Closely connected with the problems posed by the discovery of works of monumental art are certain other problems relating to the creeds and cults of the peoples of Central Asia in the pre-Moslem period. The contribution which archaeology can make to the solution of these problems is of pre-eminent importance.

I am not, however, qualified to discuss these problems in detail. In the following paragraphs I am concerned only to give a general account of the situation as it was on the eve of the Arab conquest, before the population became subject to Moslem influence. Fortunately the material now available on this period is fairly extensive, if not yet complete.

This problem has, of course, long interested scholars. Within the context of the history of the universal religions the main question at issue in Central Asia has been the place of origin of Zoroastrianism. The preponderant view both in western Europe and in the Soviet Union is that the home of Zoroaster and his doctrine is to be sought in Central Asia (Bactria, Khorezm), and that this religion was predominant among the local population. Attempts have been made, in consequence, to explain the archaeological data on the basis of certain passages in the *Avesta*, the sacred book of the Zoroastrians. Thus, for example, the female statuettes which are frequently found are interpreted as representations of Anahita, the Avestan goddess of water and the vegetable kingdom. The view is also widely held that the method of ossuary burial which is so characteristic of Central Asia is to be regarded as a Zoroastrian feature. In the author's opinion, however, neither of these propositions has been convincingly demonstrated. The case for regarding ossuary burials as evidence of Zoroastrianism seems particularly weak. A distinctive feature of the Central Asian ossuaries is the occurrence on the front of the lids of various representations of human figures and sometimes of whole scenes, and of animals and various types of ornament. With one or two exceptions we are quite unable to explain these representations on the basis of the canons of Zoroastrianism: indeed some of them are quite clearly incompatible with a Zoroastrian interpretation. Thus the scenes showing mourning for the dead which are sometimes found on the ossuaries, or the figures of women dancing a funeral dance, are in flagrant contradiction with the Avestan directions as to burial rites.

Certain features of the ossuary burial rite as it was practised in the pre-Arab period were undoubtedly of very varied origins. The scenes of mourning for the dead evidently stem from the customs of the steppe peoples, including the Scythians, which are so vividly described by many authors, from Herodotus to the Byzantine historians, and by the Chinese chroniclers. It seems probable that the use of ossuaries, and in particular the practice of decorating them with various scenes and figures, developed under the influence of the practice of burying the dead in decorated sarcophagi which was so widely diffused in the Hellenistic and late Roman periods.

We must also note that the ossuary method of burial is found in countries which have no connection with Zoroastrianism—for example in Palestine. In considering the place of Zoroastrianism among the other religions of Central Asia, too, we must observe that, in spite of the large scale of archaeological investigation, not a single temple has so far been discovered which can be identified with confidence as a fire temple; and meanwhile, as we have seen, the excavations have brought to light numbers of temples belonging to other religions. Even more significant is the fact that the written documents in the languages of the peoples of Central Asia do not contain a single text showing any connection with Zoroastrianism. These facts can scarcely be due to mere chance. And although this negative evidence is not, of course, sufficient to exclude the existence of Zoroastrianism altogether it does indicate that it cannot have been the predominant religion.

The religious situation in pre-Moslem Central Asia, as V.V. Bartold observed quite a long time ago, was marked by a considerable degree of tolerance. There is no evidence to indicate that any single religion achieved the status of an official state religion throughout the whole of Central Asia. This area, indeed, provided an asylum for the adherents of various heretical doctrines and beliefs, who were exposed to persecution in countries where there was a dominant religion officially recognised by the state—as was the case, for example, in Iran or Byzantium.

The towns of Central Asia, with a population of mixed origin and mixed social class, were the meeting place of many different ideologies and creeds and cults; and this naturally led to a process of syncretisation of these varied elements.

This trend is clearly evident in the cult buildings and the art of Pendzhikent. The two temples are of particular interest. Their most striking feature is the unusual architectural plan, to which no exact parallel has been found elsewhere, though certain similarities can be detected with, for example, a shrine at Surkh-Kotal and Buddhist temples at Ak-Bekish and in eastern Turkestan. We are clearly not entitled, however, to identify them as Zoroastrian fire temples, of the type familiar in Iran, or as Buddhist shrines.

A very varied pattern of religious beliefs is revealed also by the works of art found at Pendzhikent, both in the temples themselves and in dwelling houses. A detailed analysis of these works from the point of view of their religious affiliations would open up a very large field of study: here a few general remarks must suffice.

The remains of paintings in the temples provide evidence of the great importance attached to the cult of ancestors and its associated rituals: examples are the scene showing mourning for the dead in the second temple and the funeral banqueting and dancing scenes in the first. It is very probable that the temples themselves were mainly dedicated to this cult; and indeed we find confirmation of this in the written sources.

Other wall paintings found mainly in private houses but sometimes also in temples (e.g., the figure of a female divinity holding in her hands symbolic representations of the sun and moon) and some pieces of relief sculpture in wood (e.g., a representation of the solar chariot), together with symbolic representations of heavenly bodies on certain ossuaries and other examples of small plastic art from Central Asia, show that the heavenly bodies—the sun, the moon and the planets—had recognised symbolic representations and were objects of religious veneration.

The carved panel from the *iwân* of the second temple entitles us to suppose that there was a cult of water, which may have taken more concrete form in the worship of certain particular rivers, including the Zeravshan.

One of the most remarkable works of religious iconography at Pendzhikent is a fine representation of a four-armed female divinity which was discovered in 1964 within the precincts of the second temple *(Plate 133)*, during the excavation of the remains of structures belonging to a building horizon earlier than the temples themselves. The goddess is shown seated on a throne in the shape of a fantastic animal, a dragon with the body of a snake. There is another figure of a goddess with four arms among a group of mourners represented in a painting in the second temple. On the basis of iconographic analysis, combined with certain passages in the written sources, I have no doubt that this goddess was worshipped in Pendzhikent under the name of Nanaia, whose cult—under this or some other name—was widely diffused throughout the Near East from the remotest times. Her name is found at Pendzhikent on one of the types of coins minted locally, and one of the early Arab geographers tells us that it also formed part of the official style of the local rulers.

One work which stands almost alone among the surviving examples of the art of Pendzhikent is a representation of a divinity in the form of a dancing male figure whose body is painted blue. In all probability this figure was inspired by the iconography of Shiva, the Indian divinity whose characteristic attributes were his dancing pose and the blue colouring of his body.

It need hardly be said that this brief account of religious cults, based as it is on the surviving fragments of Central Asian art, cannot claim to be complete; but even this summary is sufficient to show how complex was the local pattern of religious beliefs. It is clear that in the symbolism associated with the iconography of the local cults we can detect elements borrowed from other areas. Thus an analysis of the symbol of the sun (Mithra) as the driver of a chariot shows that this symbol was taken over from other cults — for example, that of the Indian sun god Surya or the Greek Helios. The iconography of the goddess with four arms is similarly a mingling of quite disparate elements from the cults of India and the countries of the Near East. This syncretisation of cult images was a consequence of Central Asia's wide-ranging connections with the countries of the East and of the general tolerance of alien cults to which reference has already been made.

SYNOPTIC
CHRONOLOGIGAL TABLES

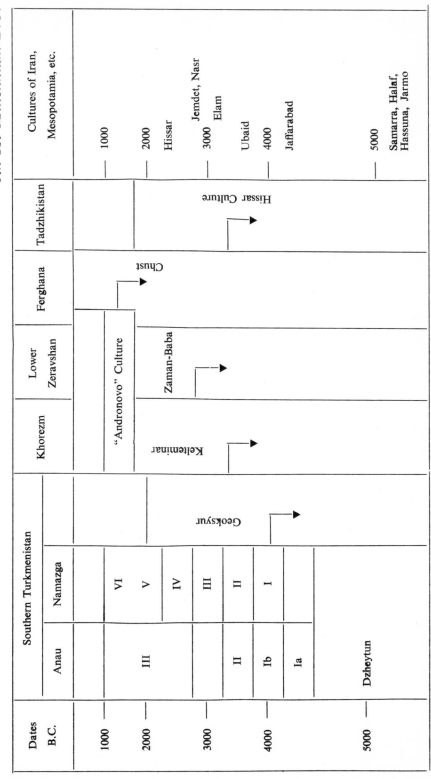

6th-1st Millennium B.C.

Dates	Central Asia	Dates	Iran
530-330 B.C.	Achaemenid satrapies in Central Asia	559-330	Achaemenid Empire
		559-529	Cyrus II, the Great
522-518	Risings in Margiana and other parts of Central Asia	522-486	Darius I
		520-518	Behistun inscription
329-327	Resistance by Bactrians, Sogdians and Sacae to Alexander the Great	334-330	Alexander the Great's conquest of the western parts of the Acheamenid possessions and Iran
		323	Alexander dies in Babylon
312-250	Seleucid satraps in Central Asia	321-64	Seleucids
c. 250-130	Greco-Bactrian kingdom	250 B.C.-226 A.D.	Parthian kingdom
c. 165	Appearance of Yueh-chi in Central Asia	c. 173-138	Mithridates I
128	Chang-k'ien in northern Bactria	c. 123-88	Mithridates II
1st cent. B.C. to 4th cent. A.D.	Kushan kingdom	53 B.C.	Parthian victory over the Romans at Carrhae
c. 25 B.C.-35 A.D.	Kujula Kadphises		
78-123	Kanishka I		
		226-651	Sassanids
c. 217-241	Vasudeva	226-241	Ardashir I
		241-273	Shapur I
c. 2nd half 3rd cent. to mid 4th cent.	Kidarites (a branch of the Kushan dynasty) and Chionites	309-379	Shapur II
359	Chionites allied with the Sassanid King Shapur II at the siege of Amida		
		End of 5th cent	Mazdakite movement
mid 5th cent. to 563/5	Kingdom of Hephthalites (White Huns)		
484	Death of the Sassanid King Peroz in battle with Hephthalites	530-579	Khusro I
563-565	End of Hephthalite kingdom. Division of its territory between the Sassanids (Khusro I) and the Turkish Kaganate		
c. 580	Split of the Turkish Kaganate into Eastern and Western Kaganates		
588-589	Bahram Chubin's war with the Turks	590	Bahram Chubin
630	Hsuan-Ts'ang in Central Asia	599-627	Khusro II
651	Capture of Merv by the Arabs	637-651	Arab conquest of Iran
674	First Arab advance into Transoxiana (Maverannakhr)		

Dates	N.W. India	Dates	China and the Northern Steppes
6th to 4th cent. B.C.	Achaemenid satrapy	Mid 7th to end 5th cent B.C.	Ch'in dynasty
364-324	Nanda dynasty in Magadha		
327-325	Alexander the Great's march to India		
324-c.200	Maurya dynasty		
273-236	Asoka		
c. 190-40	Indo-Greek kings	202 B.C.-25 A.D.	Earlier Han dynasty
		205-165	Formation of "steppe empire" of Huns (Mao-tun)
2nd half 1st cent. B.C.	Beginning of Kushan conquest of India	25-221 A.D.	Later Han dynasty
Beginning of 2nd cent. A.D.	Transfer of Kushan capital to N. India (Peshawar) by King Kanishka		
		265-420	Ch'in dynasty
320-330	Chandragupta I, founder of the Gupta dynasty		
450-455	Invasion of India by Hephthalites (Huns)	386-558	Wei dynasty in N. China
		557-581	Northern dynasties
		c. 550	Formation of Turkish Kaganate
		581-618	Sui dynasty
		618-907	T'ang dynasty

NOTES

¹ In recent years systematic excavations have been carried out at Afrosiab by an expedition from the Institute of History of the Uzbek Academy of Science under the leadership of V.A. Shishkin. In 1965 some excellently preserved wall paintings dating from the 7th or early 8th century A.D. were discovered. See V.A. Shishkin, *Afrosiab — sokrovishchnitsa drevney kultury* ("Afrosiab — a Treasure-House of Ancient Culture"), Tashkent, 1966.

² See M.S. Yusupov, *50 let Samarkandskogo muzeya, 1896-1946* ("Fifty Years of the Samarkand Museum, 1896–1946"), Samarkand, 1948.

³ A. Hrdlička, "Important Paleolithic Find in Central Asia", *Science*, New Series, 90, 1939, p. 297.

⁴ The name Geoksyur is applied to a group of settlement mounds; only the settlement known as Geoksyur I has been excavated. See I.N. Khlopin, *Geoksyurskaya gruppa poseleniy epokhi eneolita. Opyt istoricheskogo analiza* ("The Geoksyur Group of Settlements of the Eneolithic Period: a Tentative Historical Analysis"), Moscow and Leningrad, 1964.

⁵ V.V. Bartold, "K istorii persidskogo eposa" ("A note on the history of Persian epic poetry"), *Transactions of the Oriental Section of the Imperial Russian Archaeological Association*, Vol. 22, Petrograd, 1915, p. 257.

⁶ Herodotus, VII, 64 (Rawlinson's translation).

⁷ W. Tarn, *Alexander the Great*, Vol. I, Cambridge, 1948, p. 60.

⁸ D. Schlumberger and P. Bernard, "Aï Khanoum", *Bulletin de correspondance hellénique*, LXXXIX, 1965, II, p. 590. D. Schlumberger, "Aï Khanoum, une ville hellénistique en Afghanistan", *Comptes rendus de l'Académie des Inscriptions et Belles-Lettres*, 1965, I, p. 36.

⁹ A.I. Terenozhkin, "Sogd i Chach" ("Sogdiana and Chach"), *Brief Communications... of the Institute of the History of Material Culture (Soviet Academy of Science)*, Moscow and Leningrad, 1950, XXXIII, p. 156.

¹⁰ N.Y. Bichurin (Brother Hyacinthus), *Sobranie svedeniy o narodakh, obitavshikh v Sredney Azii v drevnie vremena* ("Compendium of Information on the Peoples who lived in Central Asia in Ancient Times"), II, Moscow and Leningrad, 1950, p. 152. See also *Journal of the American Oriental Society*, 37, 1917, pp. 97–8.

¹¹ Bichurin, *loc. cit.*, p. 227.

¹² Strabo, XI, viii, 2.

¹³ G.A. Pugachenkova and L.I. Rempel, *Istoriya iskusstv Uzbekistana* ("History of the Arts of Uzbekistan"), Tashkent, 1965, p. 50.

¹⁴ G.A. Pugachenkova, *Khalchayan*, Tashkent, 1966, pp. 153 ff.

¹⁵ S.P. Tolstov, *Po drevnim deltam Oksa i Yaksarta* ("In the Ancient Deltas of the Oxus and Jaxartes"), Moscow, 1962, p. 210.

¹⁶ Ammianus Marcellinus, *Res Gestae*, XIX, 1 ff.

[17] Procopius, *History of the Wars*, I, iii.

[18] Bichurin, *loc. cit.*, p. 288.

[19] W. Barthold (V.V. Bartold), *Turkestan down to the Mongol Invasion*, 2nd edition (with corrections and additions), London, 1958 (E.J.W. Gibb Memorial Series, N.S., V), pp. 180–1.

[20] For the account given here I am indebted to the archaeologists engaged in the excavations at Adzhina-Tepe, B.A. Litvinsky and T.I. Zeymal.

[21] V.A. Shishkin, *Varakhsha*, Moscow, 1963, p. 167.

[22] A.U. Pope (ed.), *A Survey of Persian Art*, Vol. IV, London and New York, 1938, Plate 145.

[23] V.V. Bartold, "Vostochno-iranskiy vopros" ("The eastern Iranian problem"), *Transactions of the Russian Academy of Material Culture*, II, Leningrad, 1922, p. 366.

[24] M.I. Rostovtzeff, "Dura and the Problem of Parthian Art", *Yale Classical Studies*, V, 1935.

[25] D. Schlumberger, "Descendants non-méditerranéens de l'art grec", *Syria*, 1960, p. 316.

[26] Mario Bussagli, *Painting of Central Asia*, Skira, Geneva, 1963, p. 43 (Chapter 3, "Piandzikent and the Influence of Sogdiana"). Cf. G. Tucci, "The Tibetan 'White sun moon' and cognate deities", *East and West*, N.S., Vol. 14, Nos. 3-4, 1963, p. 133.

SELECT BIBLIOGRAPHY

(Works which contain a bibliography are marked with an asterisk).

Abbreviations

BSOAS   Bulletin of the School of Oriental and African Studies

GAIMK   Gosudarstvennaya akademiya istorii materialnoy kultury (State Academy of the History of Material Culture)

JA   Journal Asiatique

KSIE   Kratkie soobshcheniya Instituta Etnografii AN SSSR (Brief Communications of the Institute of Etnography of the Academy of Science of the U.S.S.R.)

MDAFA   Mémoires de la Délégation Archéologique Française en Afghanistan

MIA   Materialy i issledovaniya po arkheologii SSSR (Materials and Investigations on the Archaeology of the Soviet Union)

SA   Sovetskaya Arkheologiya (Soviet Archaeology)

SE   Sovetskaya Etnografiya (Soviet Ethnography)

UzFAN   Uzbekskiy filial Akademii Nauk (Uzbek Branch of the Academy of Science)

VDI   Vestnik drevney istorii (Journal of Ancient History)

YuTAKE   Yuzhno-Turkmenskaya Arkheologicheskaya Kompleksnaya Ekspeditsiya (Southern Turkmenian Complex Archaeological Expedition)

Bibliographies, Series of Reports, General Works

Sovetskaya arkheologicheskaya literatura: Bibliografiya 1918-1940 ("Soviet Archaeological Literature: Bibliography 1918-1940"), Moscow and Leningrad, 1965.

Sovetskaya arkheologicheskaya literatura: Bibliografiya 1941-1957 ("Soviet Archaeological Literature: Bibliography 1941-1957"), Moscow and Leningrad, 1959.

Arkheologicheskie raboty v Tadzhikistane ("Archaeological Work in Tadzhikistan"), I-IX, Dushanbe, 1954-1961.

A.N. BERNSHTAM, "Istoriko-arkheologicheskie ocherki tsentralnogo Tyan-Shanya i Pamiro-Alaya" ("Historico-archaeological studies on the Central

Tien Shan and Pamiro-Alay Mountains"), *MIA*, 26, Moscow and Leningrad, 1952.

A.N. BERNSHTAM, "Trudy Semirechenskoy arkheologicheskoy ekspeditsii: Chuyskaya dolina" ("Reports of the Semirechye Archaeological Expedition: the Chu Valley"), *MIA*, 14, Moscow and Leningrad, 1950.

*G. FRUMKIN, "Archaeology in Soviet Central Asia", I-V, *Central Asian Review*, 1963-1965.

Istoriya materialnoy kultury Uzbekistana ("History of the Material Culture of Uzbekistan"), 1-7, Tashkent, 1959-1966.

*Istoriya Tadzhikskogo naroda ("History of the Tadzhik People"), Vol. I, *S drevneyshikh vremen do V v. n.e.* ("From the Earliest Times to the 5th century A.D."), Moscow, 1963.

*Istoriya Uzbekskoy SSR ("History of the Uzbek SSR"), Vol. I, Book 1, Tashkent, 1955.

Materialy Khorezmskoy ekspeditsii ("Papers of the Khorezm Expedition"), 1-7, Moscow, 1959-1963.

G.A. PUGACHENKOVA and L.I. REMPEL, *Istoriya iskusstv Uzbekistana s drevneyshikh vremen do serediny devyatnadtsatogo veka* ("History of the Arts of Uzbekistan from the Earliest Times to the Middle of the Nineteenth Century"), Moscow, 1965.

Termezskaya arkheologicheskaya ekspeditsiya ("The Termez Archaeological Expedition"), Vol. I, *Publications of UzFAN*, Series I, No. 2, Tashkent, 1941.

Termezskaya arkheologicheskaya ekspeditsiya ("The Termez Archaeological Expedition"), *Publications of the Academy of Science of the Uzbek SSR*, Series I, Vol. II, Tashkent, 1945.

S.P. TOLSTOV, *Drevniy Khorezm* ("Ancient Khorezm"), Moscow, 1948.

S.P. TOLSTOV, *Po drevnim deltam Oksa i Yaksarta* ("In the Ancient Deltas of the Oxus and Jaxartes"), Moscow, 1962.

Trudy Instituta Istorii i Arkheologii ("Publications of the Institute of History and Archaeology"), Academy of Science of the Uzbek SSR, Vols. I-VIII, Tashkent, 1948-1957.

Trudy Tadzhikskoy arkheologicheskoy ekspeditsii ("Reports of the Tadzhik Archaeological Expedition"), Vols. I-V: *MIA*, 15, 1950; 37, 1953; 66, 1958; 124, 1964; 136, 1966.

Trudy Khorezmskoy arkheologo-etnograficheskoy ekspeditsii ("Reports of the Khorezm Archaeological and Ethnographical Expedition"), Vols. I-IV, Moscow, 1952-1959.

Trudy Yuzhno-turkmenskoy arkheologicheskoy kompleksnoy ekspeditsii ("Reports of the Southern Turkmenian Complex Archaeological Expedition"), Vols. I-XII, Ashkhabad, 1949-1964.

INTRODUCTORY

**Arkheologicheskie ekspeditsii Gosudarstvennoy Akademii istorii materialnoy kultury i Instituta Arkheologii AN SSSR 1919-1956: Ukazatel* ("Archaeological Expeditions of the State Academy of the History of Material Culture and the Institute of Archaeology of the Academy of Science of the USSR: an Index"), Moscow, 1962.

Arkheologiya i estestvennye nauki ("Archaeology and the Natural Sciences"), Moscow, 1965.

P.J. KOSTROV and I.L. NOGID, "Removal of Salts from Ancient Middle Asian Painting by means of Electrodialysis", *Studies in Conservation*, Vol. 10, No. 3, August 1965.

P.J. KOSTROV and E.G. SHEININA, "Restoration of Monumental Painting on Loess Plaster using Synthetic Resins", *Studies in Conservation*, Vol. 6, Nos. 2 and 3, 1961.

B.B. LUNIN, *Iz istorii russkogo vostokovedeniya i arkheologii v Turkestane: Turkestanskiy kruzhok lyubiteley arkheologii (1895-1917 gg.)* ("A Contribution to the History of Russian Oriental Studies and Archaeology in Turkestan: the Amateur Archaeologists' Association of Turkestan, 1895 to 1917"), Tashkent, 1958.

M.E. MASSON, "Kratkiy ocherk istorii izucheniya Sredney Azii v arkheologicheskom otnoshenii" ("A Brief Survey of the History of the Archaeological Study of Central Asia"), Part I, *Publications of the Central Asian State University*, No. 81, Tashkent, 1956.

S.A. SEMENOV, "Pervobytnaya tekhnika (Opyt izucheniya drevneyshikh orudiy i izdeliy po sledam raboty)" ("Primitive Technology: a Study of the Earliest Implements and Manufactured Articles"), *MIA*, 54, 1957.

A.Y. YAKUBOVSKY, "Iz istorii arkheologicheskogo izucheniya Samarkanda" ("A Contribution to the History of the Archaeological Investigation of Samarkand"), *Publications of the Oriental Department of the State Hermitage*, Leningrad, 1940, Vol. II, pp. 285 ff.

I. PREHISTORIC CENTRAL ASIA

Kh. A. ALPYSBAEV, "Nakhodki nizhnego paleolita v yuzhnom Kazakhstane" ("Finds of Lower Palaeolithic Material in Southern Kazakhstan"), *Publications of the Institute of History, Archaeology and Ethnography of the Academy of Science of the Kazakh SSR*, Vol. 7, *Archaeology*, 1959, pp. 239-241.

A.N. BERNSHTAM, "Naskalnye izobrazheniya Saymaly-Tash" ("Rock Pictures of Saymaly-Tash"), *SE*, 1952, No. 2.

D.D. BUKINICH, "Istoriya pervobytnogo oroshaemogo zemledeliya v Zakaspiyskoy oblasti v svyazi s voprosom o proiskhozhdenii zemledeliya i skotovodstva" ("The History of Primitive Irrigation Agriculture in the Transcaspian Region in relation to the Problem of the Origin of Agriculture and Stockrearing"), *Khlopkovoe delo* ("Cotton Industry"), 1924, Nos. 3-4.

S.S. CHERNIKOV, "Rol andronovskoy kultury v istorii Sredney Azii i Kazakhstana" ("The Rôle of the Andronovo Culture in the History of Central Asia and Kazakhstan"), *KSIE*, 26, 1957.

A.A. FORMOZOV, "O naskalnykh izobrazheniyakh Zaraut-kamara v ushchelye Zaraut-say" ("The Rock Paintings of Zaraut-Kamara in the Zaraut-Say Gorge"), *SA*, 1966, 4, pp. 14 ff.

B.Z. GAMBURG and N.G. GORBUNOVA, "Novye dannye o kulture epokhi bronzy ferganskoy doliny" ("New Evidence on the Bronze Age Culture of the Ferghana Valley"), *SA*, 1957, 3.

Y.G. GULYAMOV, U. ISLAMOV and A. ASKAROV, *Pervobytnaya kultura i voznikovenie oroshaemogo zemledeliya v nizovyakh Zarafshana* ("Primitive Culture and the Emergence of Irrigation Agriculture in the Lower Zeravshan Valley"), Tashkent, 1966.

M.A. ITINA, "Stepnye plemena Sredneaziatskogo mezdurechya vo vtoroy polovine 2-go — nachale 1-go tysyacheletiya do n.e." ("The Steppe Tribes of the Central Asian Inter-River Area in the Second Half of the 2nd and the Early 1st Millennium B.C."), *25th International Congress of Orientalists: Papers presented by the Soviet Delegation*, Moscow, 1960.

I.N. KHLOPIN, *Geoksyurskaya gruppa poseleniy epokhi eneolita* ("The Geoksyur Group of Eneolithic Settlements"), Moscow and Leningrad, 1964.

B.A. KUFTIN, "Polevoy otchet o rabote XIV otryada YuTAKE po izucheniyu kultury pervobytnoobshchinnykh osedlo-zemledelcheskikh poseleniy epokhi medi i bronzy v 1952 g." ("Field Report on the Work of YuTAKE Team No. XIV on the Study of the Culture of the Primitive-Communal Settled Agricultural Population of the Copper and Bronze Ages, 1952"), *Reports of YuTAKE* Vol. VII, Ashkhabad, 1959.

B.A. LATYNIN, "Raboty v rayone proektiruemoy elektrostantsii na r. Naryn v Fergane" ("Work in the Area of the Projected Power Station on the River Naryn in Ferghana"), *Transactions of GAIMK*, No. 110, Leningrad, 1935.

D.N. LEV, "Arkheologicheskie issledovaniya Samarkandskogo Gosudarstvennogo universiteta v 1955-1956 gg." ("Archaeological Investigations of Samarkand State University in 1955-1956"), *Publications of Samarkand State University*, N.S., No. 101.

D.N. LEV, "Drevniy paleolit v Aman-Kutane" ("Early Palaeolithic at Aman-Kutan"), *Publications of the Uzbek State University*, N.S., No. 39, Samarkand, 1949.

B.A. LITVINSKY, "Namazga-tepe po dannym raskopok 1949-1950 gg." ("Namazga-Tepe: the 1949-1950 Excavations"), *SE*, 1952, No. 4.

B.A. LITVINSKY, A.P. OKLADNIKOV and V.A. RANOV, *Drevnosti Kayrak-Kumov* ("Antiquities of the Kayrakkum"), Dushanbe, 1962.

V.M. MASSON, *Srednyaya Aziya i Drevniy Vostok* ("Central Asia and the Ancient East"), Moscow and Leningrad, 1964.

A.P. OKLADNIKOV, "Drevneyshie arkheologicheskie pamyatniki Krasnovodskogo poluostrova" ("The Oldest Archaeological Sites on the Krasnovodsk Peninsula"), *Reports of YuTAKE*, II, Ashkhabad, 1953, p. 105.

R. PUMPELLY, *Explorations in Turkestan. Expedition of 1904: Prehistoric Civilisations of Anau*, Vols. I-II, Washington, 1908.

V.A. RANOV, *Kamennyy vek Tadzhikistana* ("The Stone Age in Tadzhikistan"), I, *Paleolit* ("The Palaeolithic"), Dushanbe, 1965.

V.A. RANOV, "Risunki kamennogo veka v grote Shakhty" ("Stone Age Drawings in the Shakhty Cave"), *SE*, 1961, No. 6.

A. ROGINSKAYA, *Zaraut-say*, Moscow, 1950.

V.I. SPRISHEVSKY, *Chustskoe poselenie (K istorii Fergany v epokhu bronzy)* ("The Settlement of Chust: a Contribution to the History of Ferghana in the Bronze Age") (Author's abstract), Tashkent, 1963.

*Srednyaya Aziya v epokhu kamnya i bronzy ("Central Asia in the Stone and Bronze Ages"), Moscow and Leningrad, 1966.

Teshik-Tash. Paleoliticheskiy chelovek ("Teshik-Tash and Palaeolithic Man") (Collected articles), Moscow, 1949.

H.V. VALLOIS, Review of A. OKLADNIKOV, G. DEBETS and V. GROMO-VA, "Issledovanie paleoliticheskoy peshchery Teshik-Tash" ("Investigation of the Palaeolithic Cave of Teshik-Tash"), *L'Anthropologie*, Paris, Vol. 50, 1941-1946, pp. 529-532.

F. WEIDENREICH, "The Palaeolithic Child from Teshik-Tash Cave in Southern Uzbekistan (Central Asia)", *American Journal of Physical Anthropology*, N.S., 3, 1945, pp. 151-162.

*Y.A. ZADNEPROVSKY, "Drevnezemledelcheskaya kultura Fergany" ("The Ancient Agricultural Culture of Ferghana"), *MIA*, 118, 1962.

II. CENTRAL ASIA IN THE EARLY HISTORICAL PERIODS

K.A. AKISHEV and G.A. KUSHAEV, *Drevnyaya kultura sakov i usuney doliny reki Ili* ("The Ancient Culture of the Sacae and the Wu-sun in the Valley of the River Ili"), Alma-Ata, 1963.

L.I. ALBAUM, *Balalyk-tepe*, Tashkent, 1960.

Y.D. BARUZDIN, "Kara-bulakskiy mogilnik" ("The Kara-Bulak Cemetery"), *Transactions of the Kirghiz Academy of Science*, III, 3, Frunze, 1961.

A.N. BERNSHTAM, "Kenkolskiy mogilnik" ("The Kenkol Cemetery"), *Archaeological Expeditions of the Hermitage*, 2, Leningrad, 1940.

M. le BERRE and D. SCHLUMBERGER, "Observations sur les remparts de Bactres", *MDAFA*, XIX, Paris, 1964, pp. 66 ff.

R. CURIEL and G. FUSSMAN, "Le trésor monétaire de Qunduz", *MDAFA*, XX, Paris, 1965.

O.M. DALTON, *The Treasure of the Oxus*, London, 1926.

M.M. DYAKONOV, "Slozhenie klassovogo obshchestva v Severnoy Baktrii" ("The Formation of a Class Society in Northern Bactria"), *SA*, XIX, 1954.

I.M. DYAKONOV and V.A. LIVSHITS, *Dokumenty iz Nisy, I v. do n.e.* ("Documents from Nisa of the 1st Century B.C."), Moscow, 1960.

P. GARDNER, *The Coins of the Greek and Scythic Kings in the British Museum*, London, 1886.

R. GHIRSHMAN, "Le problème de la chronologie des Kouchans", *Cahiers d'histoire mondiale*, III, Neuchâtel, 1957, pp. 689-717.

R. GHIRSHMAN, "Les Chionites-Hephtalites", *MDAFA*, XIII, 1948.

R. GÖBL, "Die Münzprägung der Kušhan", in F. Altheim and R. Stiehl, *Finanzgeschichte der Spätantike*, Frankfurt a/M., 1957.

T.V. GREK, E.G. PCHELINA and B.Y. STAVISKY, *Kara-tepe — buddiyskiy peshchernyy monastyr v Starom Termeze* ("Kara-Tepe: a Buddhist Cave Monastery in Old Termez"), Moscow, 1964.

G.V. GRIGORYEV, "Gorodishche Tali-Barzu" ("The Site of Tali-Barzu"), *Publications of the Oriental Department of the State Hermitage*, Leningrad, 1940.

G.V. GRIGORYEV, "Kelesskaya step v arkheologicheskom otnoshenii" ("The Archaeology of the Keles Steppe"), *Communications of the Academy of Science of the Kazak SSR*, No. 46, Alma-Ata, 1948.

A.V. GUDKOVA, *Tok-kala*, Tashkent, 1964.

W.B. HENNING, "The Bactrian Inscription", *BSOAS*, XIII, 1960, pp. 47-55.

Indiya v drevnosti ("India in Antiquity") (Collected articles), Moscow, 1964.

S.K. KABANOV, "Sogdiyskoe zdanie V v. n.e. v doline r. Kashka-Daryi" ("A Sogdian Building of the 5th Century A.D. in the Kashka-Darya Valley"), *SA*, 1958, No. 3. (On Aul-Tepe).

L.R. KYZLASOV, "Arkheologicheskie issledovaniya na gorodishche Ak-Beshim v 1953-1954 gg." ("Archaeological Investigations on the Site of Ak-Beshim in 1953-1954"), *Reports of the Kirghiz Archaeological and Ethnographical Expedition*, II, Moscow, 1959.

V.A. LAVROV, *Gradostroitelnaya kultura Sredney Azii* ("The Town-Building Culture of Central Asia"), Moscow, 1950.

B.A. LITVINSKY, "Arkheologicheskie otkrytiya na vostochnom Pamire i problema svyazey mezhdu Sredney Aziey, Kitaem i Indiey v drevnosti" ("Archaeological Discoveries in the Eastern Pamirs and the Problem of

Connections between Central Asia, China and India in Ancient Times"), *25th International Congress of Orientalists: Papers presented by the Soviet Delegation*, Moscow, 1960.

I.E. VAN LOHUIZEN de LEEUW, *The "Scythian" Period*, Leyden, 1949.

A.I. MANDELSHTAM, "Kochevniki na puti v Indiyu" ("The Nomads' Route into India"), *MIA*, 136, 1966.

A. MARICQ, "La grande inscription de Kaniska et l'étéotokharien, l'ancienne langue de la Bactriane", *JA*, 246, 1958, pp. 345-385.

M.E. MASSON, "Nakhodki fragmenta skulpturnogo karniza pervykh vekov n.e." ("Find of a Fragment of a Sculptured Cornice of the Early Centuries A.D."), *Papers of Uzbek Archaeological Service*, I, Tashkent, 1933.

M.E. MASSON and G.A. PUGACHENKOVA, "Mramornye statui parfyansko-go vremeni iz Staroy Nisy" ("Marble Statues of the Parthian Period from Old Nisa"), *Annual of the Institute of Art History, 1956*, Moscow, 1957, p. 477.

M.E. MASSON and G.A. PUGACHENKOVA, *Parfyanskie ritony Nisy* ("The Parthian Rhytons from Nisa"), Moscow, 1956.

V.A. MESHKERIS, *Terrakoty Samarkandskogo muzeya* ("Terracottas in the Samarkand Museum") (Catalogue), Leningrad, 1962.

A.K. NARAIN, *The Indo-Greeks*, Oxford, 1957.

E.E. NERAZIK, *Selskie poseleniya afrigidskogo Khorezma* ("Village Settlements of Afrigidian Khorezm"), Moscow, 1966.

V.A. NILSEN, *Stanovlenie feodalnoy arkhitektury Sredney Azii (V-VIII vv.)* ("The Development of the Feudal Architecture of Central Asia, 5th to 8th centuries"), Tashkent, 1966.

O.V. OBELCHENKO, "Kuyu-Mazarskiy mogilnik" ("The Kuyu-Mazarsk Cemetery"), *Publications of the Institute of History and Archaeology of the Uzbek Academy of Science*, No. 8, Tashkent, 1956.

G.A. PUGACHENKOVA, *Khalchayan*, Tashkent, 1965.

K. SHIRATORI, "A Study of Sut'e or Sogdiana", *Memoirs of the Research Department of the Toyo Bunko*, Tokyo, No. 2, 1928.

V.A. SHISHKIN, *Varakhsha*, Moscow, 1963.

O.I. SMIRNOVA, *Katalog monet s gorodishcha Pendzhikent* ("Catalogue of Coins from the City of Pendzhikent"), Moscow, 1963.

Sogdiyskie dokumenty s gory Mug ("Sogdian Documents from Mount Mug"), Nos. I-III, Moscow, 1962-1963.

Sogdiyskiy sbornik ("Sogdian Studies"), Leningrad, 1934.

B.Y. STAVISKY, "Ossuarii iz Biya-Naymana" ("Ossuaries from Biya-Nayman"), *Publications of the State Hermitage*, Vol. V, Leningrad, 1961.

W.W. TARN, *The Greeks in Bactria and India*, Cambridge, 2nd ed. 1951, reprinted 1966.

A.I. TERENOZHKIN, "Kholm Ak-tepe bliz Tashkenta" ("The Mound of Ak-Tepe near Tashkent"), *Publications of the Institute of History and Archaeology of the Uzbek Academy of Science*, No. 1, Tashkent, 1948.

C. TREVER (K.V. Trever), *Terracottas from Afrasiab*, Moscow and Leningrad, 1934.

K.V. TREVER, *Pamyatniki Greko-baktriyskogo iskusstva* ("Monuments of Greco-Bactrian Art"), Moscow and Leningrad, 1940.

M.V. VOEVODSKY and M.P. GRYAZNOV, "U-sunskie mogilniki na territorii Kirgizskoy SSR" ("Wu-sun Cemeteries in the Kirghiz SSR"), *VDI*, 1938, No. 3.

M.G. VOROBEVA, "Keramika Khorezma antichnogo perioda" ("The Pottery of Khorezm in the Ancient Period"), *Reports of the Khorezm Archaeological and Ethnographical Expedition*, IV, 1959.

V.L. VORONINA, *Problemy rannesrednevekovogo goroda Sredney Azii* ("Problems of an Early Mediaeval Town in Central Asia") (Author's abstract of doctoral dissertation), Moscow, 1961.

A.Y. YAKUBOVSKY, *Drevniy Pyandzhikent: Po sledam drevnikh kultur* ("Ancient Pyandzhikent: In the Footsteps of Ancient Cultures") (A collection of studies), Moscow, 1961.

E.V. ZEYMAL, *Kushanskoe tsarstvo po numizmaticheskim dannym* ("The Kushan Kingdom on the Evidence of the Coins") (Author's abstract), Leningrad, 1965.

Zhivopis Drevnego Pendzhikenta ("The Painting of Ancient Pendzhikent"), Moscow, 1954.

Zhivopis i skulptura Drevnego Pendzhikent ("Painting and Sculpture of Ancient Pendzhikent"), Moscow, 1959.

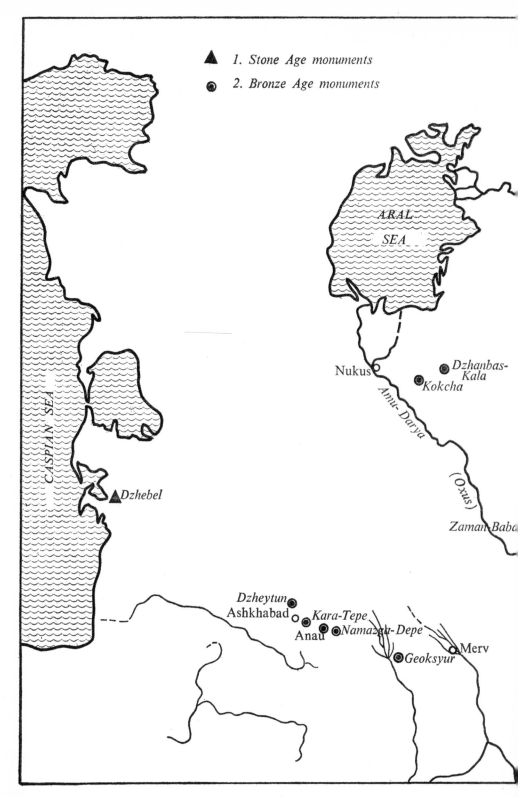

1. Stone Age monuments

2. Bronze Age monuments

ARAL SEA

CASPIAN SEA

Nukus

Amu-Darya

(Oxus)

Dzhanbas-Kala

Kokcha

Zaman Baba

Dzhebel

Dzheytun

Ashkhabad

Kara-Tepe

Anau

Namazga-Depe

Geoksyur

Merv

236

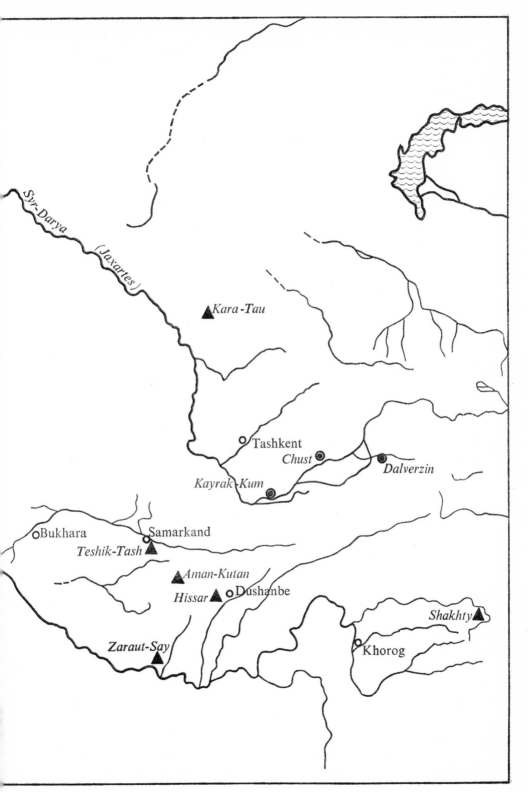

LIST OF ILLUSTRATIONS

1   *Head of Neanderthal boy. Teshik-Tash. Model by M.M. Gerasimov. (Ph. Institute of Archaeology, Leningrad).*

2   *Figurine of bovine with dappled coat. Pottery. Kara-Depe. 3rd millennium B.C.*

3   *Figurine of seated woman. Pottery. Kara-Depe. 3rd millennium B.C.*

4   *Petroglyphs (drawing). Saymaly-Tash (Ferghana). Bronze Age. (Ph. Institute of Archaeology, Leningrad).*

5   *Pottery figurines. Kara-Depe. 4th-3rd millennium B.C.*

6   *Figurine of a bull. Marble. Kara-Depe. 3rd millennium B.C.*

7   *Petroglyphs (drawing). Saymaly-Tash (Ferghana). Bronze Age. (Ph. Institute of Archaeology, Leningrad).*

8   *Plate. Pottery. Kara-Depe. 3rd millennium B.C.*

9-11   *Pottery cups. Kara-Depe. 3rd millennium B.C.*

12   *Cup. Painted pottery. Geoksyur, Turkmenistan. 4th millennium B.C.*

13   *Pottery cup. Kara-Depe. 4th-3rd millennium B.C.*

14   *Pottery vase. Takhirbay-Depe. 2nd millennium B.C.*

15-I6   *Pottery cups. Kara-Depe. 3rd millennium B.C.*

17   *Pot. Kara-Depe. 3rd millennium B.C.*

18   *Pottery vase. Yaz-Depe. 6th-4th century B.C.*

19   *Cup. Painted pottery. Sufan, Ferghana. 5th-3rd century B.C.*

20   *Pots. Yaz-Depe. 6th-4th century B.C.*

21   *Chalice. Pottery. Takhirbay-Depe. 2nd millennium B.C.*

22   *Haft of dagger. Bronze. From a Sacian funerary kurgan in the Pamirs. 6th-4th century B.C. (Ph. Institute of Archaeology, Leningrad).*

23   *Gold cup. Achaemenid work. Siberia. 5th-4th century B.C.*

24   *Phalera. Silver, partly gilded. Hellenistic work. Podgornovka, Starobelsky district, Kharkov region. 3rd-2nd century B.C.*

25   *Incense brazier. Bronze. Kazakhstan. 1st millennium B.C. (?).*

26   *Winged lion. Bronze. Semirechye. 1st millennium B.C.*

27　*Incense brazier. Bronze. Kazakhstan. 1st millennium B.C.*

28　*Yak. Bronze. Kirghizia. 1st millennium B.C.*

29　*Winged lion. Bronze. Semirechye. 1st millennium B.C.*

30　*Sacrificial dish. Bronze. Length 1.10 m.; width 1 m. Alma-Ata, Kazakhstan. 6th-4th century B.C.*

31　*Parthian art: detail of an ivory rhyton with a figure of Mars. Nisa. 2nd-1st century B.C.*

32　*Hellenistic art: silver rhyton, partly gilded. Poltava area. 3rd century B.C.*

33　*Silver cup. C. 6th-7th century A.D. Pokrovka, Semirechye, Northern Kirghizia.*

34　*Greco-Bactrian art: silver bowl decorated with hunting scenes. Vereino, Perm region. 3rd-2nd century B.C.*

35-37　*Parthian art: ivory rhytons. Nisa. 2nd-1st century B.C.*

38　*Pottery jugs. Tali-Barzu. 4th century A.D.*

39　*Pedestal cup. Pottery. Key-Kobad-Shakh. Early A.D.*

40　*Pedestal cup. Pottery. Afrosiab. Early A.D.*

41　*Handled cups. Pottery. From a tomb in Ferghana. Early 2nd century A.D.*

42　*Pedestal cup. Pottery. Afrosiab. 1st-2nd century A.D.*

43　*Handled cup. Pottery. Munchak-Tepe, Uzbekistan. 1st-2nd century A.D.*

44　*Jug, with lid. Painted pottery. Shurabashat, Ferghana. 2nd-1st century B.C.*

45　*Fragment of wall painting from Toprak-Kala. 3rd-4th century A.D.*

46　*Jars. Painted pottery. Turmiron and Dalverzin, Ferghana. Early A.D.*

47　*Fragment of ossuary. Pottery. Munchak-Tepe, Uzbekistan. 3rd-4th century A.D.*

48　*Horseman. Bronze. Verkhny Tuy Valley, Perm region. 4th-6th century A.D.*

49　*Architectural frieze on Buddhist theme. Limestone. Ayrtam, Uzbekistan. 1st century A.D.*

50　*Figure of a woman. Pottery. Toprak-Kala, Uzbekistan. 3rd-4th century A.D.*

51 *Art of Toprak-Kala: fragment of a statue, representing the head of a young man. Uzbekistan. 3rd-4th century A.D.*

52 *Anthropomorphic ossuary. Pottery. Koy-Krylgan-Kala. 1st century A.D.*

53 *Wicker basket containing a woman's toilet articles. From a tomb at Kara-Bulak, Ferghana. Early A.D.*

54 *Wooden cup. From a tomb at Kenkol. 2nd-4th century A.D.*

55 *Wicker basket. From a tomb at Kara-Bulak, Ferghana. Early A.D.*

56 *Box. Wood, with inlays. Munchak-Tepe, Uzbekistan. Early A.D.*

57 *Necklaces and other jewellery. Stone, pottery and glass. Kara-Bulak. Early A.D.*

58 *Necklaces. Glass and painted stones. Kara-Bulak. Early A.D.*

59 *Wooden cup. From a tomb at Kenkol. 2nd-4th century A.D.*

60 *Wooden dish. From a tomb at Kenkol. 2nd-4th century A.D.*

61 *Wooden table. From a tomb at Kenkol. 2nd-4th century A.D.*

62-63 *Moulds for casting ear-rings. Stone. Munchak-Tepe, Uzbekistan. Early A.D.*

64 *Stone dish. Munchak-Tepe, Uzbekistan. 1st-3rd century A.D.*

65 *Handle of a mirror in the form of a female figure. Bronze. Kara-Bulak. 3rd-4th century A.D.*

66-67 *Bronze plaques (drawings). Ak-Beshim, Semirechye. 8th century A.D.*

68 *Cup. Silver gilt. Khorezm. 5th-8th century A.D.*

69-70 *Silver cups. Khorezm. 6th-8th century A.D.*

71 *Silver ewer. Semirechye. 6th-7th century A.D.*

72 *Handled cup. Pottery. Pendzhikent. 7th-8th century A.D.*

73 *Handled cup. Pottery. Tali-Barzu. 7th-8th century A.D.*

74 *Dish. Silver gilt. Malaya Ani, Perm. 8th-10th century A.D.*

75 *Seal representing a man mounted on an elephant. Gold. Sogdian inscription with owner's name. 6th-7th century A.D.*

76 *Sogdian art: cup decorated with a scene of feasting. Silver, partly gilded. 5th-6th century A.D.*

77 *Fragment of decoration from ossuary. Pottery. Pendzhikent. 7th-8th century A.D.*

78 *Ossuary. Pottery. Samarkand. 6th-7th century A.D.*

79 *Jugs and handled cup. Pottery inlaid with mica imitating silver. Kafir-Kala. 7th century A.D.*

80 *Handled cup. Pottery. Pendzhikent. 8th century A.D.*

81 *Detail of Pl. 82*

82 *Anthropomorphic jar. Pottery. Kafir-Kala. End of 7th century A.D.*

83 *Pedestal cup. Pottery with slip. Tali-Barzu. 5th-6th century A.D.*

84 *Pottery jar. Pendzhikent. 8th century A.D.*

85 *Handled jar. Pottery. Pendzhikent. 7th century A.D.*

86 *Fragment of figurine representing a Turkish horseman. Pottery. Afrosiab. 7th to early 8th century A.D.*

87 *Figurine of a horseman. Pottery. Kafir-Kala. 7th to early 8th century A.D.*

88 *Figurines of horsemen. Pottery. Samarkand area. 7th to early 8th century A.D.*

89 *Figurine of an animal. Pottery. Samarkand area. 7th to early 8th century A.D.*

90 *Figurine of a horseman. Pottery. Samarkand area. 7th to early 8th century A.D.*

91 *Plaster cast from mould shown in Pl. 92.*

92 *Pottery mould. Kafir-Kala. 7th century A.D.*

93 *Fragment of plaster sculpture. Varakhsha. 8th century A.D.*

94 *Pottery figurines. Afrosiab. 6th-7th century A.D.*

95 *Fragment of rhyton: head of a bovine. Pottery. Afrosiab. 6th-7th century A.D.*

96 *Head of Buddha. Clay. From the Buddhist monastery of Adzhina-Tepe. 7th-8th century A.D. (Ph. Institute of History of Tadzhik Academy of Science).*

97-98	*Heads. Clay. From the Buddhist monastery of Adzhina-Tepe. 7th-8th century A.D. (Ph. Institute of History of Tadzhik Academy of Science).*
99	*Wall sculpture: woman's head. Pendzhikent. 7th-8th century A.D. (Ph. Institute of Archaeology, Leningrad).*
100	*Wall sculpture: head of Dionysus. Pendzhikent. 7th-8th century A.D. (Ph. Institute of Archaeology, Leningrad).*
101	*Wall sculpture: siren's head. Pottery. Pendzhikent. 7th-8th century A.D. (Ph. Instituteof Archaeology, Leningrad).*
102	*Wall sculpture: king playing the lyre, seated on throne flanked by two elephants. Pendzhikent. 7th-8th century A.D. (Ph. Institute of Archaeology, Leningrad).*
103	*Wall sculpture: king mounted on a camel. Pendzhikent. 7th-8th century A.D. (Ph. Institute of Archaeology, Leningrad).*
104	*Siren. Pottery. Pendzhikent. 7th-8th century A.D. (Ph. Institute of Archaeology, Leningrad).*
105	*Pottery sculpture: a fight between dragons. Pendzhikent. 7th-8th century A.D. (Ph. Institute of Archaeology, Leningrad).*
106	*Fragment of frieze with the figure of a woman. Carbonised wood. Pendzhikent. Late 7th to early 8th century A.D.*
107	*Figure of a warrior. Carbonised wood. Pendzhikent. Late 7th to early 8th century A.D.*
108	*Figure of a woman. Carbonised wood. Pendzhikent. Late 7th to early 8th century A.D.*
109	*Fragment of decorative frieze. Carbonised wood. Pendzhikent. Late 7th to early 8th century A.D.*
110	*Fragment of a shield. Wood covered with painted hide. Mount Mug. Early 8th century A.D.*
111-112	*Fragments of decorative frieze. Carbonised wood. Pendzhikent. Late 7th to early 8th century A.D.*
113	*Fragments of cloth:* above, *wool;* below, *silk. Mount Mug. Early 8th century A.D.*

114 *Fragment of decorative frieze: a family group. Carbonised wood. Pendzhi-kent. Late 7th to early 8th century A.D.*

115 *Detail of Pl. 114.*

116 *Bas-relief: triton and* makara *(a water monster). Pendzhikent. 7th-8th century A.D.*

117 *Basket lid. Wicker. Mount Mug. 7th to early 8th century A.D.*

118 *Boot. Cattle hide. Mount Mug. 7th century A.D.*

119 *Hair-net. Mount Mug. Early 8th century A.D.*

120 *Lid of ossuary. Pottery. Afrosiab. 7th-8th century A.D.*

121 *Ossuary. Pottery. Sogdiana. 7th-8th century A.D.*

122 *Wooden ladle. Mount Mug. 7th to early 8th century A.D.*

123 *Bottle. Pendzhikent. 7th-8th century A.D.*

124 *Pendzhikent excavations: street between Sector III (*on left*) and Sector XIII* (on right). *7th to early 8th century A.D. (Ph. Institute of Archaeology, Leningrad).*

125 *Pendzhikent excavations: a wall painting discovered* in situ, *representing a battle scene. Sector XXI, Room 1. (Ph. Institute of Archaeology, Leningrad).*

126 *Pendzhikent excavations: wall painting of a goddess with four arms. Second temple (northern courtyard). (Cf. Pl. 133). 6th or early 7th century A.D. (Ph. Institute of Archaeology, Leningrad).*

127 *Pendzhikent excavations: a general view of the north-eastern sector from the air. (Ph. Institute of Archaeology, Leningrad).*

128 *Pendzhikent excavations: dwelling houses in Sector III. (Ph. Institute of Archaeology, Leningrad).*

129 *Pendzhikent excavations: dwelling house in Sector XVII. (Ph. Institute of Archaeology, Leningrad).*

130 *Pendzhikent excavations: remains of vaulted roofs of two rooms in Sector III. (Ph. Institute of Archaeology, Leningrad).*

131 *Pendzhikent excavations: street between sectors III and XIII. (Ph. Institute of Archaeology, Leningrad).*

132   *Fragment of wall painting. Pendzhikent. Sector XXI, Room 1. 7th-8th century A.D.*

133   *Fragment of wall painting recovered after removal of upper layer. Four-armed goddess seated on a monster. Second temple, Pendzhikent. 6th century A.D.*

134   *Fragment of wall painting: a harp-player. Pendzhikent. 7th-8th century A.D.*

135   *Fragment of wall painting: heads of man and woman. Pendzhikent. 7th-8th century A.D.*

136   *Wall painting: the hero and his retinue setting out for war. Pendzhikent. 7th century A.D.*

137   *The same.* 1st and 2nd panels: *fight between a horseman and a monster.* 3rd panel: *after the victory.* 4th panel: *fight between horsemen.*

138   *The same.* 6th panel: *fight between demons and heroes, based on an episode in the story of Rustam in the* Shah-nama.

139   *Wall painting: a warrior mounted on an elephant is attacked by leopards. Varakhsha. 7th century A.D.*

140   *The same: an attack by griffins.*

141   *The same: an attack by tigers.*

142   *Wall painting: a banqueting scene. Pendzhikent. Sector VI, Room 1. 7th-8th century A.D.*

143   *Wall painting: a banqueting scene. Pendzhikent, Sector XVI, Room 10. 7th-8th century A.D.*

144   *The same.*

145   *The same.*

All the objects reproduced in this work are in the Hermitage Museum, Leningrad. Unless otherwise indicated, all the photographs were taken by Gérard Bertin, Geneva.

INDEX

(References in italics are to illustrations).

Achaemenid(s) 51, 53, 54, 55, 56, 57, 58, 59, 210, *23*
Adzhina-Tepe 139–42, 213, *96–98*
Afghanistan 52, 56, 75, 192, 211, 212
Afrosiab (Marakanda) 16, 17, 18, 55, 76, 98, *40, 42, 86, 94, 95, 120*
Ai-Hanum 75–6
Ak-Bekish 217
Ak-Beshim 137–8, 213, *66–67*
Akinakes 57
Ak-Tepe 116
Albaum, L.I. 116
Alexander the Great 54, 57–9, 60, 106, 210
Alexandria Eschate (Leninabad) 58
Alma-Ata *30*
Alpysbaev, Kh. 24
Aman-Kutan 24
Amazons 188
Amida 109
Ammianus Marcellinus 109
Amu-Darya, River 19, 52, 53, 75, 94, 96, 97, 98, 191
Amu-Darya Treasure 54
Amyrgian 52
Anahita 215
Anau 18, 26–7, 50
Andronovo culture 50, 191
An-si 95
Aphrodite 78
Apollo 100
Arab(s) 96, 113, 114–5, 116, 141, 155, 214, 218
Arabo-Persian 110
Aral Sea 52
Aramaic 79
Armenia(n) 110, 211
Arrian 106
Artaxerxes II 51
Artyk *30*

Aryans 192
Ashkhabad 18, 26, 27, 29, 30, 77
Asia Minor 54
Asii 95, 96
Athena 100
Aul-Tepe 116
Avesta 51, 215
Ayrtam 19, 98–9, *49*

Baba-Tag Mountains 24
Bactra (Balkh) 55, 56, 111
Bactria(n) 51, 52, 53, 55, 58, 59, 60, 75, 76, 94, 95, 96, 106, 211, 212, 215
Bactro-Sacian 52
Bagir 77
Bahram: *see* Varahran
Bahram Chubin 111
Bala-Hissar 55
Balalyk-Tepe 116, 137, 213
Balkh: *see* Bactra
Balkhash, Lake 16
Bartold, V.V. 51, 113, 216
Batyr-Tepe 116
Baysun Mountains 23
Begovat 20
Behistun (Bisutun) 51, 53
Bernshtam, A.N. 19, 20, 57
Bessus 58
Bodhisattva 139, 141
Bogatyr 188
British Museum 54
Bronze Age 18, 26, 27, 29, 30, 32, 45, 46, 48, 49, 50, 191, *4, 7*
Buddha 138, 139, 141, 142, *96*
Buddhism, Buddhist 74, 98, 99, 102, 114, 137–8, 139, 141–2, 158, 185, 212, 213, 217, *49, 96–98*
Bukhara 142, 143
Bukhar-Khudats 143

Bukinich, D.D. 29
Bussagli, M. 214
Byzantium, Byzantine 110, 111, 113, 114, 215, 216

Carrhae 101
Caspian Sea 27, 109
Chalcolithic 28
Chang-k'ien 94
Chares of Mitylene 210
Charon 106
Chavannes, E. 113
Childe, Gordon 32, 45
Chimkent 24
China, Chinese 60, 93, 94, 95, 96, 110, 111, 113, 114, 215
Chionites 109
Chi-pin 95
Chi'u-chiu-ch'ueh 95
Chorasmia: *see* Khorezm
Chorasmian language 103
Christian(ity) 114, 137, 139, 158, 185
Chust culture 47–8, 50
Ctesias 51
Cyrus 53

Dalverzin 48, *46*
Dalverzin-Tepe 75
Darius I 53
Darius III 58
Demetrius 74
Denau 75
Denike, B.P. 19
Devas 141
Diadochi 59
Dihqâns 113–4
Dionysus 79, 100, *100*
Divastich 155
Don, River 53
Dura-Europos 101, 211
Dushanbe 75, 106

Dyakonov, M.M. 74, 106
"Dynastic" art 212
Dzhanbas-Kala 45, 76
Dzhankent 16
Dzhebel Cave 27
Dzheytun 27–8, 31
Dzhumalak-Tepe 116

East, Far 50, 97
East, Near 15, 25, 26, 31, 45, 191, 218, 219
Egypt 45, 54
Eneolithic 28, 29, 30
Eucratides 93
Eurasia 98
Europoid 105

Faridun, King 137
Farkhad 20
Ferghana 47, 48, 52, 55, 60, 94, 104, 105, 116, 139, 191, *4, 7, 19, 41, 44, 46, 53, 55*
Firdausi 52, 137, 188
Fire temples 158, 217
Frada 53
Frunze 137, 142
Fu-tu 95

Gandhara 211
Gautama Buddha 141
Gaydukevich, V.F. 20
Geoksyur 28–30, *12*
Gerasimov, M.M. *1*
Greco-Bactrian 59, 60, 73–6, 93, 106, *34*
Greco-Iranian school 211
Greece, Greek(s) 54, 57–60, 74, 75, 93, 94, 95, 210
Greeks in Bactria and India (Sir W. Tarn) 60
Grigoryev, G.V. 103
Gryaznov, M.P. 19
Gulyamov, Y.G. 48
Gupta(s) 109, 110, 214

Gyaur 16
Gyaur-Kala: *see* Merv

Hatra 211
Heliocles 93
Helios 219
Hellenistic 59, 76, 77, 79, 216, *24*
Hephthalite Huns 109–12
Heraos 96
Hermitage Museum, Leningrad 21, 99, 155, 243
Herodotus 51, 52, 53, 215
Hinduism 188
Hindu Kush 96
Hindustan 110
Hissar 106
Hissar culture 46, 191
Hissar Mountains 96
Hormizd 111
Hou-han-shu 95
Hrdlička, A. 23
Hsi-tuen 95
Hsiu-mi 95
Huns 93–5, 109, 111
Huvishka 96

Imperial Archaeological Commission 16
India(n) 45, 59, 95, 98, 109, 110, 186, 192, 211, 214
Institute of Archaeology, Soviet Academy of Science 155
Institute of History, Academy of Science of Tadzhikistan 155
Iran(ian) 27, 28, 49, 51, 52, 53, 58, 59, 109, 113, 114, 115, 191, 192, 210, 211, 212, 213, 214, 216, 217
Iron Age 50
Irrigation 22, 29, 32, 46, 56, 73, 142, 209
Iwân 100, 138, 140, 143, 157, 158, 187, 217

Jarmo 28
Jaxartes: *see* Syr-Darya

Kaakhka 29
Kafir 29
Kafir-Kala *79, 81–82, 87, 91–92*
Kafirnigan, River 74
Kaftan 101, 137
Kagan(ate) 110–3
Kala 16
Kala-i-Bolo 116
Kala-i-Mir 55
Kala-i-Mug 19, 116
Kalaly-Gir 55
K'ang-kiu 60
Kanishka I 96, 97, 98
Kanishka era 97
Kao-chu 112
Kao-fu 95
Kara-Bulak *53, 55, 57, 58, 65*
Kara-Depe (Turkmenistan) 28–30, *2, 3, 5, 6, 8–11, 13, 15–17*
Karatau Mountains 24
Kara-Tepe (Uzbekistan) 99
Kashka-Darya, River 116
Kayrakkum culture 47
Kazakh(stan) 15, 19, 24, 50, 53, 191, *25, 27, 30*
Kelteminar culture 45
Kenkol *59–61*
Key-Kobad-Shakh 16, 74–5, 98, *39*
Khalchayan 99–102, 211, 212
Khāqān 111
Kharkov 24
Khayrabad-Tepe 75
Khlopin, I.N. 30
Khodzhent (Leninabad) 58
Khorezm 15, 19, 45–6, 50, 52, 53, 55, 60, 76, 102, 116, 154, 212, 215, *68–70*
Khorezm Archaeological Expedition 20

248

Khum 78, 159
Khurasan 52
Khusro I 110, 111
Khusro II 111
Kirghiz(ia) 15, 20, 112, 137, 142, *28*, *33*
Kobadian (Mikoyanabad) 54
Kokcha 46
Kostrov, P.I. 21
Koy-Krylgan-Kala 77, *52*
Krasnaya Rechka 142
Krasnovodsk 27
Kuei-shuang 95
Kuftin, B.A. 28, 29, 30
Kujula Kadphises 96
Kukhn-Kala 75
Kurgan 16, 56, 104–5, *22*
Kurgan-Tyube 139
Kurum 105
Kushan(s) 95–9, 101, 102, 106, 109, 110, 112, 114, 210, 211, 212, 213, 214
Kuva 139, 213
Kyuzeli-Gir 55–6
Kyzlasov, L.R. 137
Kyzyl-Kum desert 28, 48, 142

Lan-shi 110
Latynin, B.A. 48
Leninabad (Khodzhent) 58
Leningrad 19, 99, 243
Lerkh, P.I. 16
Lev, D.N. 24
Levina-Bulatova, V.A. 139
Liman irrigation 29
Litvinsky, B.A. 29, 47, 57, 75

Macedonian 58
Magi 114
Mahayana 139
Makara 116
Malaya Ani *74*

Maniakh 113
Manichaean, Manichaeism 114, 185
Mao-tun 93
Marakanda: *see* Afrosiab
Margiana 52, 53, 60
Marquart, J. 51
Mars *31*
Marushchenko, A.A. 27, 77
Massagetae 52, 53
Masson, M.E. 19, 20, 77, 99
Masson, V.M. 28, 30, 32, 192
Mathura 101, 211
Mazdakite movement 114
Menander 112
Merv (Gyaur-Kala) 17, 55, 114, 142
Mesolithic 25, 27
Mesopotamia 16, 28, 45, 49, 109, 191
Mihrdatkart: *see* Nisa
Mikoyanabad: *see* Kobadian
Mithra 218
Mongolia 15, 93, 113
Mongoloid 105
Monuments of Greco-Bactrian Art (K. Trever) 73
Morgan, J. de 21
Moscow 19
Moscow Scientific Centre 19
Moslem 115, 214
Mousterian 23
Mug 16
Mug, Mount 155, 185, *110, 113, 117–119, 122*
Mug-khana 105
Munchak-Tepe 20, *43, 47, 56, 62–63, 64*
Murghab, River 111

Nad-i-Ali 56, 192
Namazga-Depe 28–9, 32
Nanaia 218
Nard 189
Neanderthal 23–4, *1*

Neolithic 25, 26, 27, 28, 45, 46, 49, 191
Nestorian 139
Niaux, Grotte de 25
Nike 100, 101
Nilsen, V.A. 143
Nirvana 141, 142
Nisa (Mihrdatkart) 77–9, 102, 211, *31, 35–7*

Okladnikov, A.P. 23, 47
Ossuaries 18, 107, 215–6, 217, *52, 78, 120, 121*
Ostraca 79
Oxus, River: *see* Amu-Darya
Oxus Treasure 54, 57

Pakhsa 78, 140, 156
Palaeolithic 15, 23–5
Palestine 27, 216
Pamir-Ferghana 105
Pamirs 24, 56, 57, *22*
Panchatantra 186, 189
Paricani 52
Parthia(n) 59, 60, 78, 79, 101, 210, 211, *31, 35–37*
Parthyene 52, 53
Pasiani 95, 96
Pa-ti-yen 110
Pchelina, E.G. 99
Pekin Man 24
Pendzhikent 137, 142, 154–60, 185–9, 213, 214, 217–8, *72, 77, 80, 84, 85, 99–109, 111–112, 114–116, 123–138, 142–145*
Perm *34, 48, 74*
Peroz, King 110
Persepolis 53, 58
Persia(n): *see* Iran(ian)
Philadelphia University 18
Pliny 73
Plutarch 101
Podgornovka *24*
Pokrovka *33*

Poltava *32*
Pompeii 16
Procopius 111
Pugachenkova, G.A. 99–101, 212
Pumpelly, R. 18, 26

Quetta 192
Quintus Curtius Rufus 55

Ranov, V.A. 24–5, 46, 47
Rome, Roman 97, 101, 109, 216
Rostovtzeff, M.I. 211
Ruins of Old Merv (V.A. Zhukovsky) 17
Rustam 188, *138*
Ryasnov, I. 98

Sacae, Sacian(s) 52, 53, 56–7, 93, 95, 188, *22*
Sacarauli 95
Sai 93–4
St Petersburg 16
Saivite: *see* Shiva
Samarkand 16, 17, 24, 98, 103, 113, 155, *78*, *88–90*
Samarkand Museum 18
Sarianidi, V.I. 30
Sarv, King 137
Sassanian 109, 110, 111, 113, 115, 213, 214
Saymaly-Tash *4*, *7*
Schlumberger, D. 102, 211, 212
Schmidt, W. 18
Scythian(s) 52, 57, 104, 215
Seleucids 59
Semirechye 16, 19, 46, 93, 104, 112, 113, 137, *26*, *29*, *33*, *66–67*, *71*
Shah-nama 52, 137, 188, *138*
Shahristan 155, 157

Shakhrinau 75
Shakhty Cave 24
Shan-yu 93
Shapur II 109
Shirin-Say 20
Shishkin, V.A. 142, 144, 153
Shiva 188, 218
Shuang-mi 95
Shurabashat 55, *44*
Siberia 23, 191, *23*
Silk Road 97, 112
Skunkha 53
Sogd(ian), Sogdiana 19, 52, 55, 60, 76, 95, 103, 112, 113, 116, 155, 185, 214, *75*, *76*
Sogdo-Tadzik Archaeological Expedition 20
Southern Turkmenian Archaeological Expedition 20, 77
Sprishevsky, I.V. 48
Starobelsky *24*
Stasov, V.V. 16
Stavisky, B.Y. 99
"Steppe empire" 93, 110
Strabo 95, 96
Stupa 140, 141
Sufan *19*
Surkhan-Darya, River 75, 99
Surkh-Kotal 101, 102, 211, 212, 217
Survey of Persian Art (A.U. Pope) 210
Surya 219
Susa 21, 53
Syr-Darya, River 16, 20, 47, 53, 56, 95, 97, 101, 104, 191
Syrian 139

Tadzhik Archaeological Expedition 20
Tadzhik(istan) 15, 46, 54, 55, 60, 75, 139, 191

Ta-hia (Bactria) 94, 95, 96
Takhirbay-Depe *14*, *21*
Takhta-Karacha pass 24
Tali-Barzu 103–4, *38*, *73*, *83*
Tarkhan 113
Tarn, Sir W. 59, 60
Tashkent 18, 19, 60, 116
Ta Yueh-chi 93
Tazabagyab culture 46
Tedzhen 30
Tegiskan 56
Tell 16
Tepe 16, 142
Terenozhkin, A.I. 76
Termez 19, 23, 24, 74, 98, 99, 116
Termez Archaeological Expedition 19, 99
Teshik-Kala 116
Teshik-Tash 19, 23–4, *1*
Tibet 15
Tien Shan 56, 57, 93, 94
Tochari 95, 96
Tocharistan(ian) 96, 141
Tolstov, S.P. 19, 45, 77, 101, 102
Toprak-Kala 102–3, 212, *45*, *50*, *51*
Transcaucasia 29
Trever, K. 73
Tu-mi 95
Tup-Khona 105–6
Turfan: *see* Turkestan
Turkestan 15, 16, 50, 93, 110, 113, 185, 186, 211, 214, 217
Turk(ish) 110–2
Turkmenia, Turkmenistan 15, 26, 27, 29, 30, 45, 49, 52, 55, 76, 154, 191, *12*
Turmiron *46*
Turt-kul 16

Ubaid, Al 28
Ur 21
Urals 191

Uygarak 56, 101
Uzbekistan 15, 60, 99, 211, *43, 47, 49, 50, 51, 56, 62–63, 64*

Vakhsh, River 75, 139
Varahran V 110
Varakhsha 19, 142–4, 153–4, 213, *93, 139–141*
Vasishka 96
Vasudeva 96
Vereino *34*
Vereshchagin, V.S. 17
Verkhny-Tuy, River *48*
Veselovsky, N.I. 17
Voevodsky, M.V. 19
Volga, River 50
Voronets, E. 48

Voronina, V.L. 156
Vyatkin, V.L. 17

White Huns: *see* Hephthalite Huns
Wima Kadphises 96, 101
Woolley, Sir L. 21
Wu-sun 93–4
Wu Ti 94

Yakke-Parsan 116
Yakubovsky, A.Y. 19, 20, 155
Yang Shao culture 50
Yazdagird II 110
Yaz-Depe *18, 20*
Yeh-ta (Hephthalites) 112
Yemen 137

Yenisey, River 191
Yen-kao-chen 95
Yueh-chi 93–5, 110, 112

Zadneprovsky, Y.A. 48
Zaman-Baba culture 48–9, 50
Zang-Tepe 116
Zaraut-Say 24
Zeravshan Archaeological Expedition 19
Zeravshan Mountains 19
Zeravshan, River 48, 52, 104, 217
Zhukovsky, V.A. 17
Zhu-zhan 110
Zoroaster, Zoroastrian(ism) 51, 114, 215, 216, 217
Zyablin, L.P. 138

Printed in Switzerland

THE TEXT AND ILLUSTRATIONS
IN THIS VOLUME WERE PRINTED
ON THE PRESSES OF NAGEL
PUBLISHERS IN GENEVA.

FINISHED IN FEBRUARY 1968
BINDING BY NAGEL PUBLISHERS,
GENEVA

PLATES ENGRAVED BY CLICHÉS UNION, PARIS

LEGAL DEPOSIT No 437

PRINTED IN SWITZERLAND